C000079698

GUIDE

ISTANBUL
RESTAURANT GUIDE

RESTAURANTS, BARS AND CAFES
Your Guide to Authentic Regional Eats

GUIDE BOOK FOR TOURIST

ISTANBUL RESTAURANT GUIDE 2022
Best Rated Restaurants in Istanbul, Turkey

© Ronald F. Christopher
© E.G.P. Editorial

Printed in USA.

ISBN-13: 9798502240161

Copyright ©
All rights reserved.

ISTANBUL RESTAURANT GUIDE

The Most Recommended Restaurants in Istanbul

This directory is dedicated to Istanbul Business Owners and Managers who provide the experience that the locals and tourists enjoy. Thanks you very much for all that you do and thank for being the "People Choice".

Thanks to everyone that posts their reviews online and the amazing reviews sites that make our life easier.

The places listed in this book are the most positively reviewed and recommended by locals and travelers from around the world.

Thank you for your time and enjoy the directory that is designed with locals and tourist in mind!

TOP 500
RESTAURANTS

Ranked from #1 to #500

#1
Antakya Restaurant
Cuisines: Turkish, Seafood, Barbeque
Average price: Modest
Area: Mimar Hayrettin Mh.
Address: Mimar Hayrettin Mh.
34400 Istanbul Turkey
Phone: (0212) 5180117

#2
Varka Antakya Lezzetleri
Cuisines: Turkish, Middle Eastern
Average price: Modest
Area: Asmalı Mescit Mh.
Address: İstiklal Cad. Emir Nevruz Sok. 2 / E
34430 Istanbul Turkey
Phone: (0212) 2438927

#3
Van Kahvaltı Evi
Cuisines: Breakfast & Brunch,
Cafe, Coffee & Tea
Average price: Inexpensive
Area: Kılıçali Paşa Mh.
Address: Kılıç Ali Paşa Mah.
34433 Istanbul Turkey
Phone: (0212) 2936437

#4
Ziya Baba
Cuisines: Turkish, Chicken Wings, Kebab
Average price: Inexpensive
Area: Küçük Ayasofya Mh.
Address: Küçük Ayasofya Mh.
34200 Istanbul Turkey
Phone: (0212) 4580736

#5
Dürümzade
Cuisines: Kebab, Turkish, Wraps
Average price: Inexpensive
Area: Hüseyinağa Mh.
Address: Hüseyinağa Mah.
34435 Istanbul Turkey
Phone: (0212) 2490147

#6
Okkalı Kahve
Cuisines: Coffee & Tea, Cafe, Cafeteria
Average price: Inexpensive
Area: Sinanpaşa Mh.
Address: Ihlamurdere Cad.
34353 Istanbul Turkey
Phone: (0212) 2369506

#7
Çorlulu Ali Paşa Nargile Cafe
Cuisines: Hookah Bar, Cafe, Cafeteria
Average price: Inexpensive
Area: Mollafenari Mh.
Address: Mimar Hayrettin Mh.
34200 Istanbul Turkey
Phone: (0538) 6896367

#8
Beyti
Cuisines: Turkish
Average price: Expensive
Area: Şenlikköy Mh.
Address: Orman Sok. No: 8
34153 Istanbul Turkey
Phone: (0212) 6632990

#9
Old Ottoman Cafe & Restaurant
Cuisines: Turkish
Average price: Modest
Area: Alemdar Mh.
Address: Prof. Kazım Gürkan Cd.
34122 Istanbul Turkey
Phone: (0212) 5145500

#10
Hamdi Restaurant
Cuisines: Turkish, Cafe, Coffee & Tea
Average price: Modest
Area: Rüstem Paşa Mh.
Address: Tahmis Cad.
34116 Istanbul Turkey
Phone: (0212) 5280390

#11
Aret'in Yeri
Cuisines: Seafood, Turkish, Pubs
Average price: Modest
Area: Katip Mustafa Çelebi Mh.
Address: Katip Mustafa Çelebi Mah.
34250 Istanbul Turkey
Phone: (0212) 2921010

#12
Datlı Maya
Cuisines: Turkish, Fast Food,
Breakfast & Brunch
Average price: Modest
Area: Firuzağa Mh.
Address: Firuzağa Mah.
34425 Istanbul Turkey
Phone: (0212) 2929057

#13
Tarihi Sultanahmet Köftecisi Selim Usta
Cuisines: Turkish, Meatballs, Soup
Average price: Modest
Area: Binbirdirek Mh.
Address: Alemdar Mh.
34200 Istanbul Turkey
Phone: (0212) 5136468

#14
Hatay Has Kral Sofrası
Cuisines: Turkish
Average price: Modest
Area: İskenderpaşa Mh.
Address: Sofular Mah.
34080 Istanbul Turkey
Phone: (0212) 5349707

#15
Rotisserie Noir
Cuisines: Steakhouse, French
Average price: Expensive
Area: Bostancı Mh.
Address: Bağdat Cad. No:460
34710 Istanbul Turkey
Phone: (0216) 4451505

#16
Canım Ciğerim
Cuisines: Turkish, Giblets, Fast Food
Average price: Modest
Area: Asmalı Mescit Mh.
Address: Minare Sok. No: 1
34200 Istanbul Turkey
Phone: (0212) 2526060

#17
Cha'ya Galata
Cuisines: Cafe, Coffee & Tea, Cafeteria
Average price: Modest
Area: Şahkulu Mh.
Address: Şahkulu Bostan Sok. No:22/ A
34200 Istanbul Turkey
Phone: (0212) 2498503

#18
Latife Hanım
Cuisines: Turkish, Tapas/Small Plates
Average price: Expensive
Area: Şehit Muhtar Mh.
Address: Istiklal Cad. Bekar Sk. 22/ A
34310 Istanbul Turkey
Phone: (0212) 2930068

#19
Mangerie
Cuisines: Cafe, Cocktail Bar, Coffee & Tea
Average price: Modest
Area: Bebek Mh.
Address: Cevdet Paşa Cad. No:69
34342 Istanbul Turkey
Phone: (0212) 2635199

#20
Virginia Angus
Cuisines: Burgers, Meatballs, American
Average price: Modest
Area: Tahtakale Mh.
Address: Uzunçarşı Cad. No:136
34200 Istanbul Turkey
Phone: (0212) 5283808

#21
Derviş Baba Kahvehanesi
Cuisines: Coffee & Tea, Cafe, Cafeteria
Average price: Inexpensive
Area: Ayvansaray Mh.
Address: Sultan Çeşmesi Cad. No:79/1
34087 Istanbul Turkey
Phone: (0539) 7191959

#22
İstisna Tatlar
Cuisines: Cafe, Coffee & Tea, Cafeteria
Average price: Inexpensive
Area: Caferağa Mh.
Address: Caferaga Mah.
34200 Istanbul Turkey
Phone: (0216) 3496585

#23
Petra Roasting Co.
Cuisines: Cafe, Coffee & Tea
Average price: Modest
Area: Esentepe Mh.
Address: Panorama Selenium Residence
Mağaza 1, 34349 Istanbul Turkey
Phone: (0212) 3561053

#24
Zübeyir Ocakbaşı
Cuisines: Barbeque
Average price: Modest
Area: Şehit Muhtar Mh.
Address: Bekar Sok. No: 28
34250 Istanbul Turkey
Phone: (0212) 2933951

#25
Fıccın
Cuisines: Turkish, Mediterranean, Tapas Bar
Average price: Modest
Area: Asmalı Mescit Mh.
Address: İstiklal Cad.
34450 Istanbul Turkey
Phone: (0212) 2933786

#26
Salkım Söğüt
Cuisines: Seafood, Turkish Ravioli, Vegetarian
Average price: Inexpensive
Area: Caferağa Mh.
Address: Caaferağa Mah.
34718 Istanbul Turkey
Phone: (0216) 4506018

#27
Helvetia
Cuisines: Homemade Food, Desserts
Average price: Inexpensive
Area: Asmalı Mescit Mh.
Address: General Yazgan Sok. 8/A
34430 Istanbul Turkey
Phone: (0212) 2458780

#28
Khorasani Ocakbaşı
Cuisines: Turkish, Seafood, Barbeque
Average price: Modest
Area: Alemdar Mh.
Address: Divan Yolu Cad. Ticarethane Sok.
No: 39/41, 34200 Istanbul Turkey
Phone: (0212) 5195959

#29
Klemuri
Cuisines: Turkish, Mediterranean, Black Sea
Average price: Modest
Area: Katip Mustafa Çelebi Mh.
Address: Katip Mustafa Çelebi Mah.
34433 Istanbul Turkey
Phone: (0212) 2923272

#30
Namlı Rumeli Köftecisi
Cuisines: Meatballs
Average price: Inexpensive
Area: Hoca Paşa Mh.
Address: Hoca Paşa Mah. Ankara Cad.
34110 Istanbul Turkey
Phone: (0212) 5112196

#31
Çiğdem Pastanesi
Cuisines: Bakeries, Cafe, Coffee & Tea
Average price: Modest
Area: Binbirdirek Mh.
Address: Divanyolu Cad. No: 62/A
34500 Istanbul Turkey
Phone: (0212) 5268859

#33
Aret'in Yeri Teras
Cuisines: Turkish, Tapas/Small Plates, Tabernas
Average price: Expensive
Area: Katip Mustafa Çelebi Mh.
Address: Katip Çelebi Mah.
34433 Istanbul Turkey
Phone: (0212) 2433188

#32
Nostra Casa
Cuisines: Italian
Average price: Expensive
Area: Küçük Ayasofya Mh.
Address: K Ayasofya Cad. Mustafa Paşa
Sok. No: 42, 34149 Istanbul Turkey
Phone: (0212) 5175819

#34
Asmalimescit Dürümcüsü
Cuisines: Fast Food, Turkish, Wraps
Average price: Inexpensive
Area: Şahkulu Mh.
Address: Nergis Sok. No.2/A
34200 Istanbul Turkey
Phone: (0212) 2440802

#35
Happy Moon's
Cuisines: Italian, Tex-Mex, Mexican
Average price: Modest
Area: Fenerbahçe Mh.
Address: Fener Kalamış Cad. No:89
34726 Istanbul Turkey
Phone: (0216) 5500500

#36
Kahve 6
Cuisines: Coffee & Tea, Cafe
Average price: Modest
Area: Kılıçali Paşa Mh.
Address: Akarsu Cad.
34200 Istanbul Turkey
Phone: (0212) 2930849

#37
Yeni Lokanta
Cuisines: Homemade Food
Average price: Modest
Area: Kuloğlu Mh.
Address: Kumbaracı Yokuşu No:66
34433 Istanbul Turkey
Phone: (0212) 2922550

#38
Şehzade Erzurum Cağ Kebabı
Cuisines: Kebab
Average price: Modest
Area: Hoca Paşa Mh.
Address: Ankara Cad.
34200 Istanbul Turkey
Phone: (0212) 5203361

#39
Page Cafe & Gallery
Cuisines: Cafe, Coffee & Tea
Average price: Modest
Area: Caferağa Mh.
Address: Moda Cad. 121-1/ A
34200 Istanbul Turkey
Phone: (0532) 5410979

#40
Karadeniz Pide ve Döner Salonu
Cuisines: Turkish, Pita, Donairs
Average price: Modest
Area: Sinanpaşa Mh.
Address: Sinan Paşa Mah.
34349 Istanbul Turkey
Phone: (0212) 2617693

#41
PASAJ Cook & Book
Cuisines: Vegetarian, Homemade Food
Average price: Inexpensive
Area: Caferağa Mh.
Address: Caferağa Mh
34200 Istanbul Turkey
Phone: (0216) 4144400

#42
Kale Cafe
Cuisines: Breakfast & Brunch, Pita, Cafeteria
Average price: Modest
Area: Rumeli Hisarı Mh.
Address: Yahya Kemal Cd. No:16
34860 Istanbul Turkey
Phone: (0212) 2650097

#43
Tuzla Balıkçısı
Cuisines: Seafood
Average price: Modest
Area: Postane Mh.
Address: Manastır Yolu Cad. 6
34940 Istanbul Turkey
Phone: (0216) 3959910

#44
Vapiano
Cuisines: Italian, Bar
Average price: Modest
Area: Suadiye Mh.
Address: Bağdat Cad.Selim Ragip Emec
Sok.No.4, 34740 Istanbul Turkey
Phone: (0216) 4644265

#45
Pera Thai
Cuisines: Thai
Average price: Expensive
Area: Evliya Çelebi Mh.
Address: Evliya Çelebi Mah.
34421 Istanbul Turkey
Phone: (0212) 2455725

#46
Mikla
Cuisines: Scandinavian, Bar, Turkish
Average price: Exclusive
Area: Asmalı Mescit Mh.
Address: The Marmara Pera Hotel
34430 Istanbul Turkey
Phone: (0212) 2935656

#47
Babel Cafe & Restaurant
Cuisines: Turkish
Average price: Modest
Area: Kuloğlu Mh.
Address: Turnacıbaşı Cad. No: 56
34250 Istanbul Turkey
Phone: (0212) 2442665

#48
Giritli Restoran
Cuisines: Greek
Average price: Inexpensive
Area: Sultan Ahmet Mh.
Address: Keresteci Hakkı Sok. No: 8
34200 Istanbul Turkey
Phone: (0212) 4582270

#49
Üçüncü Mevkii
Cuisines: Turkish
Average price: Inexpensive
Area: Şehit Muhtar Mh.
Address: Hüseyinağa Mah.
34420 Istanbul Turkey
Phone: (0212) 2442223

#50
Balıkçı Sabahattin
Cuisines: Seafood
Average price: Expensive
Area: Cankurtaran Mh.
Address: Seyit Hasan Kuyu Sok. No: 1
34200 Istanbul Turkey
Phone: (0212) 4581824

#51
Tarihi Çınaraltı Aile Çay Bahçesi
Cuisines: Coffee & Tea,
Breakfast & Brunch, Cafe
Average price: Inexpensive
Area: Çengelköy Mh.
Address: Çengelköy Cad. Çınarlı Camii Sok.
No:4, 34680 Istanbul Turkey
Phone: (0216) 4221036

#52
Carluccio's
Cuisines: Italian, Desserts, Bistro
Average price: Modest
Area: Esentepe Mh.
Address: Kanyon AVM
34394 Istanbul Turkey
Phone: (0212) 3530545

#53
Barba Yani Restaurant
Cuisines: Seafood
Average price: Expensive
Area: Burgazadası Mh.
Address: Yalı Cad. No:8/A
34975 Istanbul Turkey
Phone: (0216) 3812727

#54
Limonlu Bahçe
Cuisines: Bar, Mediterranean, Turkish
Average price: Modest
Area: Tomtom Mh.
Address: Tomtom Mah. Yeniçarşı Cad.
34400 Istanbul Turkey
Phone: (0212) 2521094

#55
Set Balık Lokantası
Cuisines: Seafood, Turkish
Average price: Expensive
Area: Kireçburnu Mh.
Address: Haydar Aliyev Cad. No:18
34467 Istanbul Turkey
Phone: (0212) 2620411

#56
Bakıroğlu Peynirci Kahvaltı
Cuisines: Delicatessen, Breakfast & Brunch
Average price: Modest
Area: Bostancı Mh.
Address: Bostancı Mah.
34710 Istanbul Turkey
Phone: (0216) 3623025

#57
Topaz
Cuisines: Mediterranean, Ottoman Cuisine
Average price: Exclusive
Area: Ömer Avni Mh.
Address: Ömer Avni Mah.
34427 Istanbul Turkey
Phone: (0212) 2491001

#58
Sultanahmet Fish House
Cuisines: Turkish, Seafood
Average price: Expensive
Area: Alemdar Mh.
Address: Prof. İsmail Gürkan Cad. No: 14
34200 Istanbul Turkey
Phone: (0212) 5274445

#59
Journey
Cuisines: Mediterranean, Breakfast &
Brunch, Homemade Food
Average price: Modest
Area: Kılıçali Paşa Mh.
Address: Kılıç Ali Paşa Mah.
34290 Istanbul Turkey
Phone: (0212) 2448989

#60
Dem Karaköy
Cuisines: Coffee & Tea,
Breakfast & Brunch, Tea Rooms
Average price: Modest
Area: Kemankeş Karamustafa Paşa Mh.
Address: Kemankeş Mah.
34425 Istanbul Turkey
Phone: (0212) 2939792

#61
Ciğerci Hulusi
Cuisines: Turkish, Giblets
Average price: Modest
Area: Caferağa Mh.
Address: Caferağa Mah.
34200 Istanbul Turkey
Phone: (0216) 3361123

#62
Solera Winery
Cuisines: Beer, Wine & Spirits, Turkish
Average price: Modest
Area: Kuloğlu Mh.
Address: Yeni Çarsi Cad. No:44
34250 Istanbul Turkey
Phone: (0212) 2522719

#63
Ulus 29
Cuisines: Turkish, Bar, Gastropub
Average price: Exclusive
Area: Kuruçeşme Mh.
Address: Yol Sok. No: 71 D: 1
34400 Istanbul Turkey
Phone: (0212) 2656181

#64
Halil Lahmacun
Cuisines: Lahmacun, Soup
Average price: Inexpensive
Area: Caferağa Mh.
Address: Caferağa Mah.
34718 Istanbul Turkey
Phone: (0216) 3370123

#65
Erhan Restaurant
Cuisines: Turkish
Average price: Modest
Area: Binbirdirek Mh.
Address: Binbirdirek Mah.
34200 Istanbul Turkey
Phone: (0541) 3454949

#66
Polonez Barbekü
Cuisines: Barbeque, Turkish
Average price: Modest
Area: Caddebostan Mh.
Address: Bağdat Cad. No: 291/C
34728 Istanbul Turkey
Phone: (0216) 3023101

#67
Nicole
Cuisines: Mediterranean
Average price: Exclusive
Area: Tomtom Mh.
Address: Bogazkesen Cad. Tomtom Kaptan
Sok. No:18, 34433 Istanbul Turkey
Phone: (0212) 2924467

#68
Banyan
Cuisines: Asian Fusion
Average price: Exclusive
Area: Yıldız Mh.
Address: Muallim Naci Cad. Salhane Sok.
No.3 Istanbul Turkey
Phone: (0212) 2599060

#69
Aşşk Kahve
Cuisines: Coffee & Tea, Cafe, Turkish
Average price: Modest
Area: Kuruçeşme Mh.
Address: Kuruçeşme Mah.
34330 Istanbul Turkey
Phone: (0212) 2654734

#70
No: 19 Dining
Cuisines: Vegetarian, Homemade Food
Average price: Modest
Area: Kuloğlu Mh.
Address: Kuloğlu Mah.
34433 Istanbul Turkey
Phone: (0212) 2443513

#71
Beppe Pizzeria
Cuisines: Pizza, Italian
Average price: Modest
Area: Caferağa Mh.
Address: Caferağa Mh.
34710 Istanbul Turkey
Phone: (0216) 5502200

#72
Peymane
Cuisines: Middle Eastern,
Tapas/Small Plates, Turkish
Average price: Modest
Area: Tomtom Mh.
Address: No: 65 D: 1
34200 Istanbul Turkey
Phone: (0212) 2933136

#73
Pizzeria Pera
Cuisines: Pizza, Italian, Wine Bar
Average price: Modest
Area: Asmalı Mescit Mh.
Address: Asmalımescit Mh.
34430 Istanbul Turkey
Phone: (0212) 2438643

#74
Muhit Cafe
Cuisines: Cafe, Breakfast & Brunch,
Coffee & Tea
Average price: Modest
Area: Kemankeş Karamustafa Paşa Mh.
Address: Kemankeş Mah.
34200 Istanbul Turkey
Phone: (0212) 2436525

#75
Balkan Lokantası
Cuisines: Turkish
Average price: Inexpensive
Area: Cihannüma Mh.
Address: Akmaz Çeşme Sok. No: 8
34200 Istanbul Turkey
Phone: (0212) 5859828

#76
Fuego Restaurant
Cuisines: Turkish, Cafe, Mediterranean
Average price: Modest
Area: Alemdar Mh.
Address: Alemdar Mh.
34110 Istanbul Turkey
Phone: (0212) 5313697

#77
Dodo Cafe
Cuisines: Fast Food, Breakfast & Brunch
Average price: Modest
Area: Caferağa Mh.
Address: Moda Cad.
34710 Istanbul Turkey
Phone: (0216) 3383726

#78
Sıdıka
Cuisines: Turkish, Seafood
Average price: Expensive
Area: Sinanpaşa Mh.
Address: Vişnezade Mah.
34200 Istanbul Turkey
Phone: (0212) 2597232

#79
Neyzade Restaurant
Cuisines: Turkish
Average price: Expensive
Area: Hoca Paşa Mh.
Address: Taya Hatun Sok. No: 5
34120 Istanbul Turkey
Phone: (0212) 5284344

#80
Dürümcü Emmi
Cuisines: Kebab, Turkish, Soup
Average price: Modest
Area: Osmanağa Mh.
Address: Osmanağa Mah.
34810 Istanbul Turkey
Phone: (0216) 3481886

#81
Garda Cafe
Cuisines: Coffee & Tea,
Breakfast & Brunch, Cafe
Average price: Modest
Area: Rasimpaşa Mh.
Address: Rasimpaşa Mah.
34716 Istanbul Turkey
Phone: (0216) 4188088

#82
Pandeli Restaurant
Cuisines: Turkish
Average price: Expensive
Area: Rüstem Paşa Mh.
Address: Mısır Çarşısı No:1
34116 Istanbul Turkey
Phone: (0212) 5273909

#83
Şimşek Pide
Cuisines: Pita
Average price: Inexpensive
Area: Şehit Muhtar Mh.
Address: Şehit Muhtar Mah.
34250 Istanbul Turkey
Phone: (0212) 2494642

#84
Nusr.Et
Cuisines: Steakhouse
Average price: Expensive
Area: Etiler Mh.
Address: Nispetiye Cd. No:87
34200 Istanbul Turkey
Phone: (0212) 3583022

#85
Paşazade Restaurant
Cuisines: Turkish
Average price: Modest
Area: Hoca Paşa Mh.
Address: Hoca Paşa Mah. İbni Kemal Cad.
34200 Istanbul Turkey
Phone: (0212) 5133757

#86
Cafe Grande
Cuisines: Coffee & Tea, Cafe
Average price: Modest
Area: Alemdar Mh.
Address: Hacı Tahsinbey Sok. No: 44
Istanbul Turkey
Phone: (0212) 5127780

#87
Sur Ocakbaşı
Cuisines: Turkish, Barbeque
Average price: Modest
Area: Zeyrek Mh.
Address: No: 27
34200 Istanbul Turkey
Phone: (0212) 5338088

#88
Kanaat Lokantası
Cuisines: Turkish
Average price: Modest
Area: Sultantepe Mh.
Address: Selmanipak Cad. No:9
34674 Istanbul Turkey
Phone: (0216) 5533791

#89
Safa Meyhanesi
Cuisines: Tapas/Small Plates
Average price: Expensive
Area: Yedikule Mh.
Address: İlyas Bey Cad.
34098 Istanbul Turkey
Phone: (0212) 5855594

#90
Rumeli Meyhanesi
Cuisines: Turkish, Tapas Bar, Tabernas
Average price: Modest
Area: Asmalı Mescit Mh.
Address: Asmalımescit Mh
34344 Istanbul Turkey
Phone: (0212) 2516400

#91
Kadı Nimet Balıkçılık
Cuisines: Seafood
Average price: Modest
Area: Caferağa Mh.
Address: Serasker Cad.
34710 Istanbul Turkey
Phone: (0216) 3487389

#92
Lacivert Restoran
Cuisines: Seafood, Breakfast & Brunch
Average price: Expensive
Area: Anadolu Hisarı Mh.
Address: Körfez Cad.
34398 Istanbul Turkey
Phone: (0216) 4133753

#93
Tavanarası Restaurant
Cuisines: Pubs, Turkish
Average price: Modest
Area: Asmalı Mescit Mh.
Address: Asmalımescit Mah.
34430 Istanbul Turkey
Phone: (0212) 2442882

#94
Go Meso
Cuisines: Asian Fusion, Chinese, Barbeque
Average price: Expensive
Area: Pınar Mh.
Address: İstinye Park AVM.
34460 Istanbul Turkey
Phone: (0212) 3455888

#95
Ceviz Ağacı
Cuisines: Cafe, Turkish, Italian
Average price: Modest
Area: Koşuyolu Mh.
Address: Muhittin Üstündağ Cd. No:85
34718 Istanbul Turkey
Phone: (0216) 3391826

#96
Kazan
Cuisines: Pubs, Brasseries
Average price: Modest
Area: Sinanpaşa Mh.
Address: Beşiktaş Cd. No:35
34353 Istanbul Turkey
Phone: (0212) 2615845

#97
Develi Samatya
Cuisines: Kebab
Average price: Modest
Area: Kocamustafapaşa Mh.
Address: Gümüş Yüksük Sok. No: 7
34098 Istanbul Turkey
Phone: (0212) 5290833

#98
Ali Ocakbaşı
Cuisines: Barbeque
Average price: Exclusive
Area: Arap Cami Mh.
Address: Arap Camii Mh. Tersane Cd.
34420 Istanbul Turkey
Phone: (0212) 2931011

#99
The Upper Crust Pizzeria
Cuisines: Pizza, Italian
Average price: Modest
Area: Yıldız Mh.
Address: Yıldız Mah.
34349 Istanbul Turkey
Phone: (0212) 2275227

#100
700 Gram
Cuisines: Cafe, Breakfast & Brunch
Average price: Modest
Area: Caferağa Mh.
Address: Caferağa Mh.
34335 Istanbul Turkey
Phone: (0216) 3362366

#101
Gaziantep Burç Ocakbaşı
Cuisines: Turkish, Kebab, Barbeque
Average price: Inexpensive
Area: Beyazıt Mh.
Address: Parçacılar Sk No:12
34200 Istanbul Turkey
Phone: (0212) 5271516

#102
MOC
Cuisines: Cafe, Coffee & Tea, Cafeteria
Average price: Inexpensive
Area: Teşvikiye Mh.
Address: Şakayık Sok. No:4/A
34365 Istanbul Turkey
Phone: (0212) 2344465

#103
Kebapçı İskender
Cuisines: Kebab, Turkish
Average price: Modest
Area: Caferağa Mh.
Address: Caferağa Mah.
34200 Istanbul Turkey
Phone: (0216) 3360777

#104
Albura Kathisma
Cuisines: Turkish, Seafood, Steakhouse
Average price: Modest
Area: Cankurtaran Mh.
Address: Yeni Akbıyık Cad. No: 36-38
Istanbul Turkey
Phone: (0212) 5179031

#105
Hayvore
Cuisines: Black Sea, Homemade Food
Average price: Modest
Area: Kuloğlu Mh.
Address: İstiklal Cad.
34250 Istanbul Turkey
Phone: (0212) 2457501

#106
Eleos Restaurant-Yesilkoy
Cuisines: Pubs, Greek
Average price: Exclusive
Area: Yeşilköy Mh.
Address: Yeşilbahçe Sok. No: 9
34149 Istanbul Turkey
Phone: (0212) 6633911

#107
Pedro
Cuisines: Cocktail Bar,
Modern European, Cafeteria
Average price: Modest
Area: Caferağa Mh.
Address: Caferağa Mh.
34710 Istanbul Turkey
Phone: (0216) 4180467

#108
Vogue
Cuisines: Mediterranean, Cocktail Bar
Average price: Expensive
Area: Vişnezade Mh.
Address: Akaretler Spor Cad. No:92
34357 Istanbul Turkey
Phone: (0212) 2274404

#109
Güney Restaurant
Cuisines: Turkish
Average price: Modest
Area: Şahkulu Mh.
Address: Galata Kulesi Meydanı
34430 Istanbul Turkey
Phone: (0212) 2490393

#110
Hacı Abdullah
Cuisines: Turkish
Average price: Expensive
Area: Şehit Muhtar Mh.
Address: Hüseyin Ağa Mah. Atıf Yılmaz Cad.
34250 Istanbul Turkey
Phone: (0212) 2938561

#111
Firuzende Galata Restaurant
Cuisines: Mediterranean, Cafe, Coffee & Tea
Average price: Modest
Area: Bereketzade Mh.
Address: Bereketzade Mah.
34421 Istanbul Turkey
Phone: (0212) 2439016

#112
Zencefil
Cuisines: Vegetarian, Vegan, Cafeteria
Average price: Modest
Area: Şehit Muhtar Mh.
Address: Şehit Muhtar Mah.
34250 Istanbul Turkey
Phone: (0212) 2438234

#113
Susam Cafe & Restaurant
Cuisines: Cafe, Coffee & Tea
Average price: Modest
Area: Kılıçali Paşa Mh.
Address: Susam Sok. No: 11
34250 Istanbul Turkey
Phone: (0212) 2515995

#114
Münferit
Cuisines: Modern European,
Turkish, Gastropub
Average price: Expensive
Area: Firuzağa Mh.
Address: Yeni Çarşı Cad. No: 19
34400 Istanbul Turkey
Phone: (0212) 2525067

#115
Çanak Kebap & Katmer
Cuisines: Lahmacun, Kebab
Average price: Modest
Area: 19 Mayıs Mh.
Address: İnönü Cad. No:94
34710 Istanbul Turkey
Phone: (0216) 4459242

#116
Lades Menemen
Cuisines: Breakfast & Brunch
Average price: Inexpensive
Area: Kuloğlu Mh.
Address: Katip Çelebi Mah.
34250 Istanbul Turkey
Phone: (0212) 2513203

#117
Bistro 33
Cuisines: Lounge, Bistro, Coffee & Tea
Average price: Expensive
Area: Caddebostan Mh.
Address: Bağdat Cad.
34710 Istanbul Turkey
Phone: (0216) 4786550

#118
Salomanje Restaurant
Cuisines: Turkish, Breakfast & Brunch
Average price: Modest
Area: Harbiye Mh.
Address: Atiye Sok. Belkıs Apt. No: 4 D: 1-2
Istanbul Turkey
Phone: (0212) 3273577

#119
Nar Lokantası
Cuisines: Turkish
Average price: Exclusive
Area: Mollafenari Mh.
Address: Armaggan No: 65 K: 5
Istanbul Turkey
Phone: (0212) 5222800

#120
Naftalin K.
Cuisines: Cafe, Coffee & Tea
Average price: Inexpensive
Area: Balat Mh.
Address: Balat Mah.
34087 Istanbul Turkey
Phone: (0533) 2022768

#121
Günaydın Kasap Steak House
Cuisines: Steakhouse
Average price: Exclusive
Area: Altıntepe Mh.
Address: Altıntepe Mah. Istanbul Turkey
Phone: (0216) 5199915

#122
Burrito Shop
Cuisines: Mexican
Average price: Modest
Area: Caddebostan Mh.
Address: Bagdat Cad. No: 298
34844 Istanbul Turkey
Phone: (0216) 4114567

#123
La Vie En Rose
Cuisines: French, Desserts,
Breakfast & Brunch
Average price: Modest
Area: Yeniköy Mh.
Address: Köybaşı Cad No:80/A
34464 Istanbul Turkey
Phone: (0212) 2232382

#124
The Wrap
Cuisines: Wraps, Sandwiches, Salad
Average price: Modest
Area: Etiler Mh.
Address: Edincik Sok. No:1
34337 Istanbul Turkey
Phone: (0212) 3526632

#125
Kırıntı
Cuisines: Turkish
Average price: Inexpensive
Area: Caferağa Mh.
Address: Moda Cad. Ferit Tek Sok. 15/1
34710 Istanbul Turkey
Phone: (0216) 3460770

#126
Ecoisthan Vegan Vegetarian
Restaurant & Traveller House
Cuisines: Vegan, Vegetarian,
Breakfast & Brunch
Average price: Inexpensive
Area: Bereketzade Mh.
Address: Camekan Sok. No. 7
34200 Istanbul Turkey
Phone: (0507) 3758904

#127
Pierre Loti Kahvesi
Cuisines: Coffee & Tea, Cafe
Average price: Inexpensive
Area: Eyüp Merkez Mh.
Address: Balmumcu Sok. No: 5
34240 Istanbul Turkey
Phone: (0212) 5812696

#128
Şerbethane Cafe & Restoran
Cuisines: Turkish, Coffee & Tea, Cafe
Average price: Modest
Area: Sultan Ahmet Mh.
Address: Küçükayasofya Cad.
34200 Istanbul Turkey
Phone: (0212) 5170004

#129
Uludağ Kebapçısı
Cemal & Cemil Usta
Cuisines: Turkish
Average price: Modest
Area: Küçükbakkalköy Mh.
Address: No: 39
34710 Istanbul Turkey
Phone: (0216) 5749998

#130
It's Ok.
Cuisines: Coffee & Tea, Cafe
Average price: Modest
Area: Kılıçali Paşa Mh.
Address: Kılıçali Paşa Mah.
34425 Istanbul Turkey
Phone: (0533) 5254594

#131
Aşkana Mantı
Cuisines: Turkish Ravioli
Average price: Inexpensive
Area: Nisbetiye Mh.
Address: Ulus Mah. Ahmet Adnan Saygun
Cd. 34700 Istanbul Turkey
Phone: (0212) 2687442

#132
Balkon Restaurant & Bar
Cuisines: Turkish, Cocktail Bar, Pizza
Average price: Modest
Area: Asmalı Mescit Mh.
Address: Asmalımescit Mah.
34430 Istanbul Turkey
Phone: (0212) 2932052

#133
Namlı Gurme Karaköy
Cuisines: Delis, Turkish, Breakfast & Brunch
Average price: Modest
Area: Kemankeş Karamustafa Paşa Mh.
Address: Rihtim Cad. No:1/1
34844 Istanbul Turkey
Phone: (0212) 2936880

#134
Fazıl Bey'in Türk Kahvesi
Cuisines: Coffee & Tea, Cafe,
Coffee Roasteries
Average price: Inexpensive
Area: Caferağa Mh.
Address: Serasker Cd. No:1/A
34200 Istanbul Turkey
Phone: (0216) 4502870

#135
Şeyhmuz Kebap Evi
Cuisines: Kebab
Average price: Modest
Area: Mollafenari Mh.
Address: Mollafenari Mah.
34122 Istanbul Turkey
Phone: (0212) 5261613

#136
Bafetto
Cuisines: Pizza
Average price: Modest
Area: Suadiye Mh.
Address: Bağdat Cad.No: 384/B
34728 Istanbul Turkey
Phone: (0216) 3601207

#137
Forneria
Cuisines: Turkish, Italian, Mediterranean
Average price: Modest
Area: Müeyyedzade Mh.
Address: The Haze Hotel
34425 Istanbul Turkey
Phone: (0212) 2524848

#138
Ortaklar Iskender Kebap
Cuisines: Kebab, Pita
Average price: Inexpensive
Area: Binbirdirek Mh.
Address: Binbirdirek Mah.
34200 Istanbul Turkey
Phone: (0212) 5176198

#139
Pizano Pizzeria
Cuisines: Pizza, Desserts, Italian
Average price: Modest
Area: Mecidiye Mh.
Address: Mecidiye Mah.
34
347 Istanbul Turkey
Phone: (0212) 2583035

#140
Mozaik Restaurant
Cuisines: Turkish
Average price: Modest
Area: Alemdar Mh.
Address: Divan Yolu Cad.
İncili Çavuş Sok. No: 1
34200 Istanbul Turkey
Phone: (0212) 5124177

#141
Bağ Pastanesi
Cuisines: Bakeries, Cafe, Coffee & Tea
Average price: Modest
Area: Altunizade Mh.
Address: Kısıklı Cad. No. 7
34662 Istanbul Turkey
Phone: (0216) 4740818

#142
Corner Irish Pub
Cuisines: Burgers, Irish Pub,
Beer, Wine & Spirits
Average price: Modest
Area: Sururi Mehmet Efendi Mh.
Address: Asmalı Mescit Mh.
34435 Istanbul Turkey
Phone: (0212) 2444820

#143
Big Chefs
Cuisines: Cafe, Brasseries, Coffee & Tea
Average price: Expensive
Area: Göksu Mh.
Address: Küçüksu Cad. No.4
34980 Istanbul Turkey
Phone: (0216) 3089328

#144
Buhara Restaurant
Cuisines: Turkish, Barbeque, Bar
Average price: Modest
Area: Mollafenari Mh.
Address: Nuruosmaniye Cad. No 7
34200 Istanbul Turkey
Phone: (0212) 5137424

#145
Hebun Çorba Evi
Cuisines: Soup
Average price: Inexpensive
Area: Kemankeş Karamustafa Paşa Mh.
Address: Kemankeş Karamustafa Paşa Mh.
34200 Istanbul Turkey
Phone: (0531) 6378517

#146
Moda Çay Bahçesi
Cuisines: Coffee & Tea, Cafe, Parks
Average price: Inexpensive
Area: Caferağa Mh.
Address: Ferit Tek Sok.
34710 Istanbul Turkey
Phone: (0216) 3379986

#147
Kanatçı Haydar
Cuisines: Chicken Wings, Bar, Meatballs
Average price: Modest
Area: Kocasinan Merkez Mh.
Address: Kocasinan Mrk. Mh.
34192 Istanbul Turkey
Phone: (0212) 4510454

#148
Sultan Köşesi
Cuisines: Turkish, Cafe, Coffee & Tea
Average price: Modest
Area: Sultan Ahmet Mh.
Address: Küçük Ayasofya Cad. No: 6
34122 Istanbul Turkey
Phone: (0212) 5166606

#149
Vodina Cafe
Cuisines: Coffee & Tea, Cafe, Turkish Ravioli
Average price: Modest
Area: Balat Mh.
Address: Vodina Cad. No: 41
34200 Istanbul Turkey
Phone: (0212) 5310067

#150
Shorba
Cuisines: Soup
Average price: Inexpensive
Area: Ataşehir Atatürk Mh.
Address: Arkadlı Çarşı Ata Plaza 3 No: 3 D: 5
Istanbul Turkey
Phone: (0216) 4564922

#151
Anjelique
Cuisines: Mediterranean, Dance Club
Average price: Expensive
Area: Yıldız Mh.
Address: Salhane Sok. No: 5 Istanbul Turkey
Phone: (0212) 3272844

#152
Agora Meyhanesi
Cuisines: Turkish
Average price: Expensive
Area: Ayvansaray Mh.
Address: Mürsel Paşa Cad. No: 185
34200 Istanbul Turkey
Phone: (0212) 6312136

#153
Dönerci Celal Usta
Cuisines: Donairs, Wraps
Average price: Modest
Area: İstiklal Mh.
Address: Atakent Mah.
34510 Istanbul Turkey
Phone: (0216) 3293540

#154
Midpoint
Cuisines: Coffee & Tea, Turkish, Cafe
Average price: Modest
Area: Tomtom Mh.
Address: İstiklal Cad. No.187
34200 Istanbul Turkey
Phone: (0212) 2457040

#155
Velvet Cafe
Cuisines: Cafe, Breakfast & Brunch,
Coffee & Tea
Average price: Inexpensive
Area: Arap Cami Mh.
Address: Bereketzade Mh.
34421 Istanbul Turkey
Phone: (0507) 8673761

#156
Cahide 3D
Cuisines: Turkish, Music Venues
Average price: Exclusive
Area: Vişnezade Mh.
Address: No: 19 Istanbul Turkey
Phone: (0212) 2196530

#157
Ciğeristan
Cuisines: Giblets
Average price: Modest
Area: İskenderpaşa Mh.
Address: Sofular Mah.
34200 Istanbul Turkey
Phone: (0534) 0575151

#158
Plus Kitchen
Cuisines: Salad, Sandwiches,
Breakfast & Brunch
Average price: Modest
Area: Mecidiyeköy Mh.
Address: Trump Towers AVM
34200 Istanbul Turkey
Phone: (0212) 2134173

#159
Foça Fish Gourmet
Cuisines: Seafood
Average price: Exclusive
Area: Küçükbakkalköy Mh.
Address: Küçük Bakkalköy Mah. Ahmet
Yesevi Cad. 34758 Istanbul Turkey
Phone: (0216) 5778686

#160
Lucca
Cuisines: Bar, American, Tapas/Small Plates
Average price: Expensive
Area: Bebek Mh.
Address: Bebek Mh.Cevdet Pasa Cad.
No:51 34342 Istanbul Turkey
Phone: (0212) 2571255

#161
Sinop Mantı
Cuisines: Turkish Ravioli, Desserts
Average price: Inexpensive
Area: Sinanpaşa Mh.
Address: Köprü Sok. Tellioğlu İş Hanı No: 8
D: 1 Istanbul Turkey
Phone: (0212) 2610374

#162
Siirt Şeref Büryan
Cuisines: Turkish, Soup, Giblets
Average price: Modest
Area: Zeyrek Mh.
Address: No: 4 Istanbul Turkey
Phone: (0212) 6358085

#163
Kırıntı
Cuisines: Burgers, Cafe, Coffee & Tea
Average price: Modest
Area: Caddebostan Mh.
Address: Bağdat Cad. Istanbul Turkey
Phone: (0216) 3566468

#164
Tatbak
Cuisines: Kebab, Pita, Lahmacun
Average price: Modest
Area: Teşvikiye Mh.
Address: Vali Konağı Cad.
34250 Istanbul Turkey
Phone: (0212) 2461306

#165
Mangal Keyfi
Cuisines: Kebab, Turkish
Average price: Inexpensive
Area: Şehit Muhtar Mh.
Address: Öğüt Sok. No: 8 Istanbul Turkey
Phone: (0212) 2451534

#166
Emirgan Sütiş
Cuisines: Turkish, Sandwiches
Average price: Modest
Area: Emirgan Mh.
Address: Emirgan Mah.
34510 Istanbul Turkey
Phone: (0212) 3235030

#167
Unter
Cuisines: Cafe, Gastropub,
Breakfast & Brunch
Average price: Modest
Area: Kemankeş Karamustafa Paşa Mh.
Address: Kemankes Mah.
34429 Istanbul Turkey
Phone: (0212) 2445151

#168
Lider Pide
Cuisines: Pita
Average price: Modest
Area: Ihlamurkuyu Mh.
Address: Ihlamurkuyu Mah.
34771 Istanbul Turkey
Phone: (0216) 5266361

#169
Adanalı Yusuf Usta
Cuisines: Turkish, Barbeque
Average price: Modest
Area: Cihangir Mh.
Address: Ambarlı Sofu Sok. No.14
34510 Istanbul Turkey
Phone: (0212) 4228954

#170
Litera Restaurant
Cuisines: Lounge, Turkish
Average price: Modest
Area: Tomtom Mh.
Address: Yeni Çarşı Cad. No:32
34250 Istanbul Turkey
Phone: (0212) 2928947

#171
Neolokal
Cuisines: Turkish
Average price: Expensive
Area: Arap Cami Mh.
Address: Salt Galata
34420 Istanbul Turkey
Phone: (0212) 2440016

#172
Cafe Lumiere
Cuisines: Cafe, Coffee & Tea
Average price: Inexpensive
Area: Kuloğlu Mh.
Address: Kuloğlu Mah.
34060 Istanbul Turkey
Phone: (0212) 2441267

#173
Beymen Brasserie
Cuisines: French, Bar, Brasseries
Average price: Expensive
Area: Harbiye Mh.
Address: Abdi İpekçi Cad. No: 23 D: 1
34400 Istanbul Turkey
Phone: (0212) 3430443

#174
Ara Kafe
Cuisines: Coffee & Tea, Cafe
Average price: Modest
Area: Tomtom Mh.
Address: Tomtom Mh.
34250 Istanbul Turkey
Phone: (0212) 2454105

#175
Borsam Taş Fırın
Cuisines: Pita, Lahmacun
Average price: Inexpensive
Area: Osmanağa Mh.
Address: Osmanağa Mah. Rıhtım Cad.
34400 Istanbul Turkey
Phone: (0216) 3308619

#176
Sunset Grill & Bar
Cuisines: Sushi Bar, American, Turkish
Average price: Expensive
Area: Kuruçeşme Mh.
Address: Adnan Saygun Cad. Yol Sok. Ulus
Parki No. 2. 34200 Istanbul Turkey
Phone: (0212) 2870357

#177
The House Cafe
Cuisines: Cafe, Turkish, Coffee & Tea
Average price: Modest
Area: Yıldız Mh.
Address: Salhane Sok. No: 1
34400 Istanbul Turkey
Phone: (0212) 2272699

#178
Passenger Cafe & Bistro
Cuisines: Bistro, Cafe, Bar
Average price: Modest
Area: Caferağa Mh.
Address: Caferağa Mah. Moda Cad.
34710 Istanbul Turkey
Phone: (0216) 3361757

#179
Trattoria Enzo
Cuisines: Italian
Average price: Expensive
Area: Acıbadem Mh.
Address: Akasya AVM
34660 Istanbul Turkey
Phone: (0216) 5106890

#180
Süt Yumurta Reçel
Cuisines: Breakfast & Brunch
Average price: Inexpensive
Area: Osmanağa Mh.
Address: Bahariye Ali Suavi Sok. No:30
34714 Istanbul Turkey
Phone: (0216) 3309626

#181
Hazzo Pulo Şarap Evi
Cuisines: Wine Bar, Seafood, Fast Food
Average price: Modest
Area: Asmalı Mescit Mh.
Address: Meşrutiyet Cad. No:75
34400 Istanbul Turkey
Phone: (0212) 2455523

#182
Can Oba Restaurant
Cuisines: Turkish, Seafood, German
Average price: Expensive
Area: Hoca Paşa Mh.
Address: Hoca Paşa Sok. No: 10
34112 Istanbul Turkey
Phone: (0212) 5221215

#183
Mythos Meyhane
Cuisines: Tapas/Small Plates, Beer,
Wine & Spirits, Tabernas
Average price: Expensive
Area: Rasimpaşa Mh.
Address: Tren Garı
34716 Istanbul Turkey
Phone: (0216) 3370979

#184
Cookshop
Cuisines: Turkish, Cafe, Coffee & Tea
Average price: Modest
Area: Harbiye Mh.
Address: Harbiye Mah.
34400 Istanbul Turkey
Phone: (0212) 2320566

#185
Tıkıntı Cafe
Cuisines: Cafe, Turkish, Coffee & Tea
Average price: Inexpensive
Area: Cihannüma Mh.
Address: Cihannüma Mah.
34353 Istanbul Turkey
Phone: (0212) 2274841

#186
Frankie Istanbul - The Sofa Hotel
Cuisines: Mediterranean, Lounge,
Music Venues
Average price: Exclusive
Area: Mecidiyeköy Mh.
Address: Tesvikiye Cad. 41-41/A K.8
34367 Istanbul Turkey
Phone: (0212) 2306666

#187
Yanyalı Fehmi Lokantası
Cuisines: Turkish
Average price: Modest
Area: Osmanağa Mh.
Address: Osmanağa Mah. Söğütlüçeşme
Cad. 34714 Istanbul Turkey
Phone: (0216) 3363333

#188
Gezi İstanbul
Cuisines: Bakeries, Cafe, Coffee & Tea
Average price: Modest
Area: Gümüşsuyu Mh.
Address: İnönü Cad. No: 5
34250 Istanbul Turkey
Phone: (0212) 2925353

#189
Kandilli Balıkçısı Suna Abla
Cuisines: Seafood
Average price: Expensive
Area: Kandilli Mh.
Address: No: 4 D: 17
34672 Istanbul Turkey
Phone: (0216) 3323241

#190
Bibuçuk
Cuisines: Turkish, American
Average price: Modest
Area: Caddebostan Mh.
Address: Bağdat Cad. 298/ 1-2
34724 Istanbul Turkey
Phone: (0216) 4677050

#191
Ayvalık Feneryolu Balıkçısı
Cuisines: Seafood
Average price: Expensive
Area: Fenerbahçe Mh.
Address: Bağdat Cad. No:142/ A
34844 Istanbul Turkey
Phone: (0216) 5508001

#192
Baltazar
Cuisines: Steakhouse, Barbeque, Burgers
Average price: Modest
Area: Kemankeş Karamustafa Paşa Mh.
Address: Kemankeş Karamustafa Paşa Mh.
34200 Istanbul Turkey
Phone: (0212) 2436442

#193
Leb-i Derya
Cuisines: Turkish
Average price: Expensive
Area: Sultan Ahmet Mh.
Address: Kumbaracı Yokuşu Kumbaracı Han
No: 57 D: 6 Istanbul Turkey
Phone: (0212) 2934989

#194
Mini Eatery
Cuisines: Fast Food, Burgers
Average price: Modest
Area: Caferağa Mh.
Address: Caferağa Mah.
34710 Istanbul Turkey
Phone: (0216) 3365999

#195
P. F. Chang's
Cuisines: Chinese, Sushi Bar
Average price: Expensive
Area: Etiler Mh.
Address: Etiler Mah.
34330 Istanbul Turkey
Phone: (0212) 3586060

#196
Ranchero
Cuisines: Mexican
Average price: Modest
Area: Bostancı Mh.
Address: Suadiye Mah.
34710 Istanbul Turkey
Phone: (0216) 3806500

#197
Mirror Restaurant & Bar
Cuisines: Italian, Japanese, Sushi Bar
Average price: Expensive
Area: Suadiye Mh.
Address: A Blok K: 2
34265 Istanbul Turkey
Phone: (0216) 4642710

#198
J. Burger & Kafeterya
Cuisines: Fast Food, Burgers
Average price: Modest
Area: Caddebostan Mh.
Address: Cemil Topuzlu Cad. No: 51
34710 Istanbul Turkey
Phone: (0216) 3694970

#199
360 İstanbul Restaurant
Cuisines: Dance Club, Turkish, Cocktail Bar
Average price: Expensive
Area: Tomtom Mh.
Address: İstiklal Cad. No: 163
34435 Istanbul Turkey
Phone: (0212) 2511042

#200
Zamane Kahvesi
Cuisines: Cafe, Coffee & Tea
Average price: Modest
Area: Harbiye Mh.
Address: Vali Konağı Cad. No:85 D:1
34400 Istanbul Turkey
Phone: (0212) 2960151

#201
Şair Leyla Bistro
Cuisines: Wine Bar, Beer,
Wine & Spirits, Bistro
Average price: Modest
Area: Sinanpaşa Mh.
Address: Şair Leyla Sok.
34860 Istanbul Turkey
Phone: (0212) 2592924

#202
Hala Mantı
Cuisines: Turkish Ravioli
Average price: Inexpensive
Area: Kuloğlu Mh.
Address: Kuloğlu Mah.
34250 Istanbul Turkey
Phone: (0212) 2927004

#203
Olivia's Pizzeria
Cuisines: Pizza, Italian
Average price: Modest
Area: Göztepe Mh.
Address: Bağdat Cad. No:215
34730 Istanbul Turkey
Phone: (0216) 3552438

#204
Yer
Cuisines: Cafe, Gastropub, Coffee & Tea
Average price: Modest
Area: Caferağa Mh.
Address: Caferağa Mah.
34710 Istanbul Turkey
Phone: (0216) 4501675

#205
Heybe Kafe
Cuisines: Cafe, Coffee & Tea, Desserts
Average price: Modest
Area: İslambey Mh.
Address: İslambey Mah. Halit Paşa Cad.
34240 Istanbul Turkey
Phone: (0212) 5326105

#206
Bej
Cuisines: Turkish, Modern European, Diners
Average price: Expensive
Area: Kemankeş Karamustafa Paşa Mh.
Address: Fransız Geçidi İş Mrk.
Istanbul Turkey
Phone: (0212) 2517195

#207
Tarihi Eminönü Balık Ekmek
Cuisines: Seafood, Fish & Chips
Average price: Inexpensive
Area: Rüstem Paşa Mh.
Address: Galata Köprüsü No:28
34421 Istanbul Turkey
Phone: (0212) 5289580

#208
Dönerci Ali Usta
Cuisines: Donairs, Wraps
Average price: Modest
Area: Cevizli Mh.
Address: Tugay Yolu Zuhal Cad. No:59
34846 Istanbul Turkey
Phone: (0543) 3004444

#209
Akademi 1971 Kitabevi
Cafe & Kütüphane
Cuisines: Libraries, Coffee & Tea, Cafe
Average price: Modest
Area: Caferağa Mh.
Address: Sakız Sok. No:12
34718 Istanbul Turkey
Phone: (0216) 7001971

#210
Namlı Kebap
Cuisines: Wraps, Kebab, Food Stands
Average price: Inexpensive
Area: Dikilitaş Mh.
Address: Hakkı Yeten Cad.
34349 Istanbul Turkey
Phone: (0212) 2407932

#211
Cafe De Paris
Cuisines: French
Average price: Expensive
Area: Caddebostan Mh.
Address: Bağdat Cad. Suadiye
34710 Istanbul Turkey
Phone: (0216) 4781751

#212
Gram
Cuisines: Mediterranean
Average price: Modest
Area: Asmalı Mescit Mh.
Address: Asmalı Mescit Mah.
34400 Istanbul Turkey
Phone: (0212) 2431048

#213
Kuru Kahveci Selim
Cuisines: Coffee & Tea, Cafe
Average price: Inexpensive
Area: Caferağa Mh.
Address: Caferağa Mh.
34710 Istanbul Turkey
Phone: (0532) 2568880

#214
Konyalılar Etli Ekmek Fırın Kebap
Cuisines: Turkish, Pita
Average price: Inexpensive
Area: 19 Mayıs Mh.
Address: Şemsettin Günaltay Cad. No: 150/G
34710 Istanbul Turkey
Phone: (0216) 3699999

#215
Yufka Dürüm İşleri
Cuisines: Turkish
Average price: Inexpensive
Area: Teşvikiye Mh.
Address: Teşvikiye Mah.
34400 Istanbul Turkey
Phone: (0212) 2415050

#216
Müz
Cuisines: Cafe, Florists, Coffee & Tea
Average price: Inexpensive
Area: Tomtom Mh.
Address: Hayriye Cad. No:18-A
34425 Istanbul Turkey
Phone: (0212) 2432262

#217
Modapark
Cuisines: Brasseries
Average price: Modest
Area: Caferağa Mh.
Address: Caferağa Mh.
34710 Istanbul Turkey
Phone: (0216) 4491388

#218
Miss Pizza
Cuisines: Pizza, Italian
Average price: Modest
Area: Evliya Çelebi Mh.
Address: Meşrutiyet Cad. Istanbul Turkey
Phone: (0212) 2513234

#219
Marmelat
Cuisines: Breakfast & Brunch,
Coffee & Tea
Average price: Modest
Area: Bereketzade Mh.
Address: Bereketzade Mah.
34421 Istanbul Turkey
Phone: (0212) 2444533

#220
Uskumru
Cuisines: Seafood
Average price: Expensive
Area: Anadolu Hisarı Mh.
Address: Körfez Cad. No: 55
34398 Istanbul Turkey
Phone: (0216) 4601000

#221
Dürümce
Cuisines: Wraps, Kebab
Average price: Inexpensive
Area: Yıldız Mh.
Address: Ortaköy Mah.
34349 Istanbul Turkey
Phone: (0212) 2603036

#222
Lido Restaurant
Cuisines: Seafood
Average price: Modest
Area: Büyükada-Maden Mh.
Address: Maden Mah.
34970 Istanbul Turkey
Phone: (0216) 3824309

#223
Juliet Rooms & Kitchen
Cuisines: Hostels, Cafe
Average price: Modest
Area: Caferağa Mh.
Address: Caferaga Mah.
34200 Istanbul Turkey
Phone: (0216) 3487000

#224
Cook Shop
Cuisines: Cafe, Breakfast & Brunch,
Sandwiches
Average price: Modest
Area: Caddebostan Mh.
Address: Bağdat Cad.
34710 Istanbul Turkey
Phone: (0216) 3553953

#225
Vagabondo's
Cuisines: Italian
Average price: Modest
Area: Yeniköy Mh.
Address: No: 278 Istanbul Turkey
Phone: (0212) 2990054

#226
Neo Classic
Cuisines: Bar, Cafe, Coffee & Tea
Average price: Modest
Area: Kuloğlu Mh.
Address: Örs Turistik İş Mrk.
Istanbul Turkey
Phone: (0212) 2924813

#227
Kırıntı
Cuisines: Fast Food
Average price: Modest
Area: Bebek Mh.
Address: Cevdet Paşa Cad. No: 35
34200 Istanbul Turkey
Phone: (0212) 2576727

#228
Karaköyüm
Cuisines: Turkish, Cafe
Average price: Modest
Area: Müeyyedzade Mh.
Address: Kemeraltı Cad.No. 8
34424 Istanbul Turkey
Phone: (0212) 2446808

#229
Happy Moon's Şaşkınbakkal Köşk
Cuisines: Italian, Tex-Mex, Mexican
Average price: Modest
Area: Suadiye Mh.
Address: Suadiye Mah.
34710 Istanbul Turkey
Phone: (0216) 4117273

#230
Kiraz Bahçe
Cuisines: Turkish
Average price: Modest
Area: Yeni Çamlıca Mh.
Address: Site Mah. Cevahir Cad.
34760 Istanbul Turkey
Phone: (0216) 5336603

#231
Galata Evi
Cuisines: Modern European
Average price: Expensive
Area: Bereketzade Mh.
Address: Galata Kulesi Sok. No: 15
34200 Istanbul Turkey
Phone: (0212) 2451861

#232
Tapasuma
Cuisines: Turkish, Mediterranean, Cocktail Bar
Average price: Exclusive
Area: Çengelköy Mh.
Address: Çengelköy Mh.
34680 Istanbul Turkey
Phone: (0216) 4011333

#233
Sancho Panza
Cuisines: Cafe, Coffee & Tea
Average price: Inexpensive
Area: Rasimpaşa Mh.
Address: Rasimpaşa Mah. Karakolhane Cad.
34716 Istanbul Turkey
Phone: (0216) 4503388

#234
Zahir Restaurant
Cuisines: Turkish, Breakfast & Brunch
Average price: Inexpensive
Area: Kuzguncuk Mh.
Address: Kuzguncuk Mah.
34674 Istanbul Turkey
Phone: (0216) 3100302

#235
Shake Shack
Cuisines: American, Fast Food, Burgers
Average price: Modest
Area: Acıbadem Mh.
Address: Akasya AVM
34660 Istanbul Turkey
Phone: (0216) 5105448

#236
Maria'nın Bahçesi
Cuisines: Seafood
Average price: Expensive
Area: Akat Mh.
Address: Yeşim Sok. No: 7 Istanbul Turkey
Phone: (0212) 3522626

#237
Birlik Kasap & Steakpoint
Cuisines: Steakhouse
Average price: Expensive
Area: Rüzgarlıbahçe Mh.
Address: Rüzgarlıbahçe Mah.
34805 Istanbul Turkey
Phone: (0216) 4255528

#238
Tag Cafe & Bistro
Cuisines: Bar, Cafe, Turkish
Average price: Modest
Area: Tomtom Mh.
Address: İstiklal Cad.
34433 Istanbul Turkey
Phone: (0212) 2436862

#239
İnciraltı Meyhanesi
Cuisines: Bar, Breakfast & Brunch, Turkish
Average price: Modest
Area: Beylerbeyi Mh.
Address: Arabacılar Sok. No: 4
34676 Istanbul Turkey
Phone: (0216) 5576686

#240
Fresco Cafe & Restaurante
Cuisines: Mediterranean
Average price: Modest
Area: Rüzgarlıbahçe Mh.
Address: Rüzgarlıbahçe Mah
34815 Istanbul Turkey
Phone: (0216) 4134415

#241
Suda Kebap
Cuisines: Turkish
Average price: Exclusive
Area: Galatasaray Adası
Address: Galatasaray adası Istanbul Turkey
Phone: (0212) 2634485

#242
Özgür Şef'in Deli Kasap
Cuisines: Steakhouse, Burgers
Average price: Modest
Area: Kavacık Mh.
Address: Kavacık Mah.
34800 Istanbul Turkey
Phone: (0216) 6932999

#243
Franz Kafka Cafe
Cuisines: Coffee & Tea, Cafe
Average price: Modest
Area: Sinanpaşa Mh.
Address: Sinanpaşa Mah.
34353 Istanbul Turkey
Phone: (0212) 2593126

#244
San Marco's Cafe
Cuisines: Italian, Cafe
Average price: Modest
Area: Zeytinlik Mh.
Address: Zeytinlik Mah.
34140 Istanbul Turkey
Phone: (0212) 6608020

#245
Juno
Cuisines: Mediterranean, Cafe
Average price: Modest
Area: Harbiye Mh.
Address: Mim Kemal Öke Cad. No: 15
34400 Istanbul Turkey
Phone: (0212) 2915723

#246
Yeniköy Emek Cafe
Cuisines: Breakfast & Brunch,
Coffee & Tea
Average price: Inexpensive
Area: Yeniköy Mh.
Address: Köybaşı Cd.
34464 Istanbul Turkey
Phone: (0212) 2237728

#247
Miyabi
Cuisines: Sushi Bar, Japanese
Average price: Exclusive
Area: Akat Mh.
Address: Zeytinoğlu Caddesi Yaren Sokak
6/14-15. 34335 Istanbul Turkey
Phone: (0212) 3520222

#248
Eataly
Cuisines: Italian, Grocery
Average price: Modest
Area: Levazım Mh.
Address: Zorlu Center - Meydan Katı
34340 Istanbul Turkey
Phone: (0212) 3366600

#249
180 Coffee Bakery
Cuisines: Cafe, Coffee & Tea
Average price: Inexpensive
Area: Caferağa Mh.
Address: Doktor Esat Işık Cad.
34200 Istanbul Turkey
Phone: (0216) 3375727

#250
Matbah Restaurant Ottoman Palace Cuisine
Cuisines: Turkish, Vegetarian
Average price: Expensive
Area: Cankurtaran Mh.
Address: Ottoman Hotel Imperial
34122 Istanbul Turkey
Phone: (0212) 5146151

#251
Ca'd'oro
Cuisines: Turkish
Average price: Exclusive
Area: Arap Cami Mh.
Address: No: 11
34200 Istanbul Turkey
Phone: (0212) 2438292

#252
5. Kat Cafe Bar Restaurant
Cuisines: Bar, Turkish, Coffee & Tea
Average price: Expensive
Area: Cihangir Mh.
Address: Soğancı Sok. No: 3 D: 5
34250 Istanbul Turkey
Phone: (0212) 2933774

#253
Mihrimah Sultan
Cuisines: Turkish, Breakfast & Brunch
Average price: Modest
Area: Şahkulu Mh.
Address: Kumbaracı Yokuşu No: 77 41700
Istanbul Turkey
Phone: (0212) 2936627

#254
Palatium Cafe & Restaurant
Cuisines: Turkish
Average price: Modest
Area: Cankurtaran Mh.
Address: Cankurtaran Mah.
34200 Istanbul Turkey
Phone: (0212) 5165132

#255
Simat Türk Mutfağı
Cuisines: Turkish
Average price: Modest
Area: Tepeören OSB
Address: İstanbul Tuzla Organize San. Bölg.
34538 Istanbul Turkey
Phone: (0216) 2905110

#256
360 İstanbul Suada Club
Cuisines: Bar, Turkish
Average price: Exclusive
Area: Galatasaray Adası
Address: Kuruçeşme Mh.
34345 Istanbul Turkey
Phone: (0212) 2636623

#257
Kybele Cafe
Cuisines: Cafe, Coffee & Tea
Average price: Modest
Area: Alemdar Mh.
Address: Kybele Hotel
34110 Istanbul Turkey
Phone: (0212) 5117766

#258
Balıkçı Lokantası
Cuisines: Seafood
Average price: Modest
Area: Rasimpaşa Mh.
Address: Rıhtım Cad. Teyyareci Sami Sk.
No: 20/1. 34716 Istanbul Turkey
Phone: (0216) 3464014

#259
Müzedechanga
Cuisines: Mediterranean, Bar, Turkish
Average price: Expensive
Area: Emirgan Mh.
Address: Sakıp Sabancı Cad. No: 42
34467 Istanbul Turkey
Phone: (0212) 3230901

#260
Et Mekan Steak House
Cuisines: Steakhouse, Hookah Bar, Burgers
Average price: Modest
Area: Küçük Çamlıca Mh.
Address: Küçükçamlıca Mah.
34398 Istanbul Turkey
Phone: (0216) 3261636

#261
Vino Steak House
Cuisines: Steakhouse, Bar, Italian
Average price: Expensive
Area: Göztepe Mh.
Address: Tütüncü Mehmet Efendi Cd. No:1/1
34730 Istanbul Turkey
Phone: (0216) 3630203

#262
Udonya Restaurant
Cuisines: Japanese
Average price: Expensive
Area: Kocatepe Mh.
Address: Point Otel No: 2 Istanbul Turkey
Phone: (0212) 2569318

#263
Pizza East
Cuisines: Pizza, Cocktail Bar
Average price: Expensive
Area: Vişnezade Mh.
Address: Süleyman Seba Cd. No:22
Akaretler. 34357 Istanbul Turkey
Phone: (0212) 2592259

#264
Güvenç Konyalı
Cuisines: Turkish
Average price: Modest
Area: Hoca Paşa Mh.
Address: Hoca Paşa Hamam Sok. No: 4
34200 Istanbul Turkey
Phone: (0212) 5275220

#265
The Populist
Cuisines: Gastropub
Average price: Expensive
Area: Merkez Mh.
Address: Silahşör Cad.
34384 Istanbul Turkey
Phone: (0212) 2962034

#266
Feriye Lokantası
Cuisines: Turkish
Average price: Modest
Area: Yıldız Mh.
Address: Çırağan Cad. No: 40
34200 Istanbul Turkey
Phone: (0212) 2272216

#267
Meat House Restaurant
Cuisines: Turkish
Average price: Modest
Area: Cankurtaran Mh.
Address: Seyit Hasan Sok. No: 22
34200 Istanbul Turkey
Phone: (0212) 4586863

#268
Kör Agop
Cuisines: Cafe, Coffee & Tea
Average price: Expensive
Area: Muhsine Hatun Mh.
Address: Ördekli Bakkal Sok. No: 7
34200 Istanbul Turkey
Phone: (0212) 5172334

#269
Miss Pizza
Cuisines: Pizza
Average price: Modest
Area: Kılıçali Paşa Mh.
Address: Cihangir Mah.
34430 Istanbul Turkey
Phone: (0212) 2513279

#270
Mr Cook
Cuisines: Mediterranean, Seafood, Turkish
Average price: Modest
Area: Alemdar Mh.
Address: Alemdar Mh.
34200 Istanbul Turkey
Phone: (0212) 5224846

#271
Ayaspaşa Rus Lokantası
Cuisines: Russian
Average price: Expensive
Area: Gümüşsuyu Mh.
Address: Gümüşsuyu Mah.
34437 Istanbul Turkey
Phone: (0212) 2434892

#272
St. Regis Brasserie
Cuisines: French, Turkish, Brasseries
Average price: Exclusive
Area: Harbiye Mh.
Address: The St. Regis
34367 Istanbul Turkey
Phone: (0212) 3680836

#273
Bop!
Cuisines: Breakfast & Brunch,
Coffee & Tea, Cafe
Average price: Modest
Area: Rasimpaşa Mh.
Address: Rasimpaşa Mh.
34720 Istanbul Turkey
Phone: (0216) 7001086

#274
İstanbul Modern Cafe & Restaurant
Cuisines: Mediterranean
Average price: Expensive
Area: Kılıçali Paşa Mh.
Address: Liman İşletmeleri Sahası Meclisi
Mebusan Cad. No: 4
34433 Istanbul Turkey
Phone: (0212) 2922612

#275
Spago
Cuisines: Italian, Lounge
Average price: Exclusive
Area: Kültür Mh.
Address: The St. Regis
34367 Istanbul Turkey
Phone: (0212) 3680808

#276
ZerafEt Restaurant
Cuisines: Kebab, Turkish, Pita
Average price: Expensive
Area: Kültür Mh.
Address: Ulus Mah.
34340 Istanbul Turkey
Phone: (0212) 3526075

#277
Kantin
Cuisines: Turkish, Desserts
Average price: Expensive
Area: Teşvikiye Mh.
Address: Akkavak Sok. No: 30
34400 Istanbul Turkey
Phone: (0212) 2193114

#278
Shake Shack
Cuisines: Burgers, Fast Food, American
Average price: Inexpensive
Area: Asmalı Mescit Mh.
Address: Şahkulu Mah.
34200 Istanbul Turkey
Phone: (0212) 2934552

#279
Balıkçınız Eser
Cuisines: Seafood
Average price: Modest
Area: Barbaros Mh.
Address: Barbaros Mah.
34746 Istanbul Turkey
Phone: (0216) 4707677

#280
Semolina Kafe & Restoran
Cuisines: Mediterranean, Italian, Bistro
Average price: Modest
Area: Caferağa Mh.
Address: Ressam Şeref Akdik Sok. No: 7/A
34660 Istanbul Turkey
Phone: (0216) 3308606

#281
Mavi Balık
Cuisines: Seafood
Average price: Exclusive
Area: Kuruçeşme Mh.
Address: Muallim Naci Cad. No: 64 / A
34200 Istanbul Turkey
Phone: (0212) 2655480

#282
Galata Kitchen
Cuisines: Turkish, Vegan, Vegetarian
Average price: Inexpensive
Area: Müeyyedzade Mh.
Address: Tatar Beyi Sok. No:9
34400 Istanbul Turkey
Phone: (0212) 2522022

#283
Çaykovski Cafe
Cuisines: Coffee & Tea, Cafe
Average price: Inexpensive
Area: Merkez Mh.
Address: Merkez Mah.
34394 Istanbul Turkey
Phone: (0212) 2913313

#284
Grandma
Cuisines: Coffee & Tea, Bakeries, Cafe
Average price: Modest
Area: Teşvikiye Mh.
Address: Ahmet Fetgari Sok. No 38. Kapi 5
34400 Istanbul Turkey
Phone: (0212) 2347420

#285
Cafe Firuz
Cuisines: Coffee & Tea, Cafe, Turkish
Average price: Modest
Area: Firuzağa Mh.
Address: Defterdar Yokuşu No: 55
34333 Istanbul Turkey
Phone: (0212) 2520241

#286
Lokma
Cuisines: Turkish
Average price: Modest
Area: Rumeli Hisarı Mh.
Address: Yahya Kemal Cad. No: 18
34398 Istanbul Turkey
Phone: (0212) 2657171

#287
Suat Usta 33 Mersin Tantuni
Cuisines: Wraps
Average price: Inexpensive
Area: Katip Mustafa Çelebi Mh.
Address: Katip Mustafa Çelebi Mah.
34400 Istanbul Turkey
Phone: (0212) 2925977

#288
Özkonak
Cuisines: Turkish, Desserts
Average price: Inexpensive
Area: Kılıçali Paşa Mh.
Address: Kılıçali Paşa Mah.
34440 Istanbul Turkey
Phone: (0212) 2491307

#289
Kısmet Muhallebicisi
Cuisines: Turkish
Average price: Inexpensive
Area: Hoca Gıyasettin Mh.
Address: No: 68
34200 Istanbul Turkey
Phone: (0212) 5136773

#290
Misina Balık & Restaurant
Cuisines: Seafood, Mediterranean
Average price: Expensive
Area: Fenerbahçe Mh.
Address: Fenerbahçe Mah.
34726 Istanbul Turkey
Phone: (0216) 5500258

#291
İkonium
Cuisines: Pita
Average price: Modest
Area: Nisbetiye Mh.
Address: Nisbepiye Mah.
34330 Istanbul Turkey
Phone: (0212) 2696982

#292
Cibalikapı Balıkçısı
Cuisines: Seafood
Average price: Modest
Area: Caferağa Mh.
Address: Moda Cad. Tarihi Moda İskelesi
Yolu. 34200 Istanbul Turkey
Phone: (0216) 3489363

#293
Beylerbeyi Paşa Kokoreç ve İşkembe Salonu
Cuisines: Turkish, Giblets, Fast Food
Average price: Inexpensive
Area: Çengelköy Mh.
Address: No: 53
34680 Istanbul Turkey
Phone: (0216) 3181280

#294
The Crepe Escape
Cuisines: Cafe, Creperies, Coffee & Tea
Average price: Inexpensive
Area: Suadiye Mh.
Address: Bağdat Cad.
34728 Istanbul Turkey
Phone: (0216) 4082300

#295
Holy Cafe
Cuisines: Coffee & Tea, Cafe, Sandwiches
Average price: Inexpensive
Area: Kuloğlu Mh.
Address: Çukurcuma Antikacılar Çarşısı
34250 Istanbul Turkey
Phone: (0533) 6266252

#296
Tuşba Uzman Mezeci
Cuisines: Delis
Average price: Inexpensive
Area: Cumhuriyet Mh.
Address: Ergenekon Cad. No: 27/A
34400 Istanbul Turkey
Phone: (0212) 2471342

#297
Rumelihisarı İskele Restaurant
Cuisines: Seafood
Average price: Expensive
Area: Emirgan Mh.
Address: Yahya Kemal Caddesi No:1
34398 Istanbul Turkey
Phone: (0212) 2632997

#298
Rock N Rolla
Cuisines: Pubs, Cafe, Coffee & Tea
Average price: Modest
Area: Caferağa Mh.
Address: Caferağa Mh.
34710 Istanbul Turkey
Phone: (0216) 4147141

#299
Parle
Cuisines: French
Average price: Exclusive
Area: Levazım Mh.
Address: Zorlu Center
34200 Istanbul Turkey
Phone: (0212) 3536340

#300
Nomads Restaurant
Cuisines: Middle Eastern, Music Venues
Average price: Expensive
Area: Ortaköy Mh.
Address: Muallim Naci Cad. No: 65
Istanbul Turkey
Phone: (0212) 2580777

#301
Mephisto Kitabevi & Kafe
Cuisines: Bookstores, Music & DVDs, Cafe
Average price: Modest
Area: Kuloğlu Mh.
Address: İstiklal Cd. No:125
34250 Istanbul Turkey
Phone: (0212) 2490696

#302
Tarihi Merkezefendi Köftecisi Rahmi Usta
Cuisines: Meatballs
Average price: Inexpensive
Area: Merkezefendi Mh.
Address: Merkezefendi Mah. Merkezefendi Cad. 34015 Istanbul Turkey
Phone: (0212) 5467680

#303
Günaydın Kasap & Steak House
Cuisines: Steakhouse
Average price: Expensive
Area: Pınar Mh.
Address: İstinye Park AVM
34464 Istanbul Turkey
Phone: (0212) 3455781

#304
Benusen
Cuisines: Seafood, Pubs, Tapas Bar
Average price: Expensive
Area: Caferağa Mh.
Address: Caferağa Mah.
34710 Istanbul Turkey
Phone: (0216) 3388418

#305
Köfteci Hüseyin
Cuisines: Meatballs
Average price: Inexpensive
Area: Şehit Muhtar Mh.
Address: Şehit Muhtar Mah. İstiklal Cad.
34250 Istanbul Turkey
Phone: (0212) 2437637

#306
Avam Kahvesi
Cuisines: Turkish, Italian, Fast Food
Average price: Inexpensive
Area: Katip Mustafa Çelebi Mh.
Address: Katip Mustafa Çelebi Mah.
34433 Istanbul Turkey
Phone: (0212) 2927276

#307
Tazele
Cuisines: Turkish Ravioli, Soup, Diners
Average price: Modest
Area: Esentepe Mh.
Address: Kanyon AVM
34394 Istanbul Turkey
Phone: (0212) 3535051

#308
Metet Közde Döner
Cuisines: Turkish, Kebab, Donairs
Average price: Modest
Area: Kuzguncuk Mh.
Address: İcadiye Cad. No: 39
34674 Istanbul Turkey
Phone: (0216) 5533333

#309
Tarantula
Cuisines: Gastropub
Average price: Modest
Area: Caferağa Mh.
Address: Caferağa Mah
34710 Istanbul Turkey
Phone: (0216) 4182246

#310
Antebi Kebap
Cuisines: Turkish
Average price: Modest
Area: Acıbadem Mh.
Address: Acıbadem Cad.
34660 Istanbul Turkey
Phone: (0216) 3407820

#311
Cezayir Restaurant
Cuisines: Mediterranean, Lounge
Average price: Expensive
Area: Firuzağa Mh.
Address: Hayriye Cad. No: 12
34425 Istanbul Turkey
Phone: (0212) 2459980

#312
Pudding Shop Lale Restaurant
Cuisines: Turkish, Desserts
Average price: Inexpensive
Area: Alemdar Mh.
Address: Divan Yolu Cad. No: 6
34200 Istanbul Turkey
Phone: (0212) 5222970

#313
Gaziantepli Mehmet Usta
Cuisines: Kebab, Turkish
Average price: Inexpensive
Area: Cerrahpaşa Mh.
Address: Koca Mustafa Paşa Cad.No: 126/A
34200 Istanbul Turkey
Phone: (0212) 5881606

#314
Hai! Sushi
Cuisines: Asian Fusion, Sushi Bar
Average price: Exclusive
Area: Fenerbahçe Mh.
Address: Amiral Fahri Korutürk Yat Limanı
34726 Istanbul Turkey
Phone: (0216) 5410354

#315
Nalia Karadeniz Mutfağı
Cuisines: Black Sea
Average price: Modest
Area: Bağlar Mh.
Address: No: 2 D: 3
34500 Istanbul Turkey
Phone: (0212) 6300690

#316
Adapazarı Islama Köftecisi AKO
Cuisines: Turkish, Meatballs
Average price: Modest
Area: Osmanağa Mh.
Address: Osmanağa Mah.
34200 Istanbul Turkey
Phone: (0216) 3387815

#317
Tribeca
Cuisines: Cafe, Lounge, American
Average price: Modest
Area: Teşvikiye Mh.
Address: Şakayık Sk. No:69/B
34400 Istanbul Turkey
Phone: (0212) 2308294

#318
Ehlitat Lokantası
Cuisines: Turkish
Average price: Inexpensive
Area: Şehit Muhtar Mh.
Address: Hüseyinağa Mah. İstiklal Cad.
34435 Istanbul Turkey
Phone: (0212) 2494492

#319
Şimdi Cafe
Cuisines: Cafe, Coffee & Tea
Average price: Modest
Area: Asmalı Mescit Mh.
Address: Asmalı Mescit Sok. Atlas Apt. No: 5
34200 Istanbul Turkey
Phone: (0212) 2525443

#320
Filizler Köftecisi
Cuisines: Meatballs
Average price: Modest
Area: Aziz Mahmut Hüdayi Mh.
Address: Harem Sahil Yolu No:61
34672 Istanbul Turkey
Phone: (0216) 3420000

#321
Emine Ana Tantuni
Cuisines: Turkish
Average price: Inexpensive
Area: Katip Mustafa Çelebi Mh.
Address: Sıraselviler Cad. Billurcu Sok. No:
5/A. 34250 Istanbul Turkey
Phone: (0212) 2928430

#322
Kirpi Cafe
Cuisines: Cafe, Coffee & Tea
Average price: Modest
Area: Koşuyolu Mh.
Address: Mehmet Akman Sok. No: 31
34718 Istanbul Turkey
Phone: (0216) 3390905

#323
Moshonis
Cuisines: Seafood, Turkish
Average price: Expensive
Area: Feneryolu Mh.
Address: Feneryolu Mah.
34200 Istanbul Turkey
Phone: (0216) 3491656

#324
Mitara Cafe & Art
Cuisines: Coffee & Tea, Vegetarian, Cafe
Average price: Expensive
Area: Küçük Ayasofya Mh.
Address: Küçük Ayasofya Mah.
34122 Istanbul Turkey
Phone: (0212) 6384480

#325
My Chef
Cuisines: Asian Fusion
Average price: Modest
Area: Caferağa Mh.
Address: Sakızgülü Sokak. No:24 Kadıköy
34785 Istanbul Turkey
Phone: (0216) 3304587

#326
Ergene Uzunköprü Köftecisi
Cuisines: Meatballs
Average price: Modest
Area: Türkali Mh.
Address: Nüzhetiye Cad. No: 66
34200 Istanbul Turkey
Phone: (0212) 2277676

#327
Gazi Mangal Izgara Salonu
Cuisines: Turkish
Average price: Inexpensive
Area: Şehremini Mh.
Address: Millet Cad.
34200 Istanbul Turkey
Phone: (0212) 5859276

#328
The Bite Coffeeshop
Cuisines: Desserts, Coffee & Tea, Cafe
Average price: Inexpensive
Area: Tomtom Mh.
Address: Tomtom Mah.
34433 Istanbul Turkey
Phone: (0530) 3419595

#329
Burger Joint
Cuisines: Burgers
Average price: Inexpensive
Area: Türkali Mh.
Address: Ihlamurdere Cad. No: 94
34330 Istanbul Turkey
Phone: (0212) 2587275

#330
Casita
Cuisines: Turkish Ravioli, Homemade Food
Average price: Modest
Area: Harbiye Mh.
Address: Abdi İpekçi Cad.
34400 Istanbul Turkey
Phone: (0212) 3278293

#331
Ali Haydar İkinci Bahar
Cuisines: Kebab, Turkish
Average price: Modest
Area: Kocamustafapaşa Mh.
Address: Gümüş Yüksük Sok. No: 6
34098 Istanbul Turkey
Phone: (0212) 5842162

#332
Burger Bar
Cuisines: Burgers
Average price: Modest
Area: Reşitpaşa Mh.
Address: Reşit Paşa Mah.
34467 Istanbul Turkey
Phone: (0212) 2296092

#333
BTA
Cuisines: Bistro
Average price: Modest
Area: Yeşilköy Mh.
Address: Atatürk Havalimanı Dış Hatlar
Terminalinde
34831 Istanbul Turkey
Phone: (0212) 4654141

#334
Sos Cafe
Cuisines: Cafe, Homemade Food
Average price: Inexpensive
Area: İçerenköy Mh.
Address: İçerenköy Mh.
34752 Istanbul Turkey
Phone: (0216) 5731173

#335
Borsa Restaurant
Cuisines: Turkish, Kebab
Average price: Expensive
Area: Harbiye Mh.
Address: Lütfi Kırdar Uluslararası Kongre ve
Sergi Sarayı. 34367 Istanbul Turkey
Phone: (0212) 2324201

#336
Kırçiçeği
Cuisines: Turkish, Pita, Soup
Average price: Modest
Area: Ortaköy Mh.
Address: No: 41
34200 Istanbul Turkey
Phone: (0212) 2603535

#337
Mica Pizza & Wine
Cuisines: Cafe, Coffee & Tea
Average price: Modest
Area: Tomtom Mh.
Address: Tom Tom Sokak No:5
34400 Istanbul Turkey
Phone: (0212) 2931174

#338
Bosphorus Brewing Company
Cuisines: Gastropub
Average price: Expensive
Area: Esentepe Mh.
Address: Esentepe Mah.
34330 Istanbul Turkey
Phone: (0212) 2748713

#339
Ayı
Cuisines: Bar, Wine & Spirits, Gastropub
Average price: Modest
Area: Caferağa Mh.
Address: Caferağa Mh.
34200 Istanbul Turkey
Phone: (0216) 4184476

#340
Savoy Balık
Cuisines: Seafood
Average price: Expensive
Area: Cihangir Mh.
Address: Sıraselviler Cad.
34250 Istanbul Turkey
Phone: (0212) 2493382

#341
Murat Muhallebicisi
Cuisines: Cafe, Desserts, Breakfast & Brunch
Average price: Modest
Area: Kemankeş Karamustafa Paşa Mh.
Address: Kemankeş Karamustafa Paşa Mah.
34200 Istanbul Turkey
Phone: (0212) 2451949

#342
Çömlek
Cuisines: Turkish
Average price: Modest
Area: Kısıklı Mh.
Address: Turistik Çamlıca Cad.No: 28
34398 Istanbul Turkey
Phone: (0216) 3351434

#343
Any Istanbul
Cuisines: Lounge, Cafe, Coffee & Tea
Average price: Expensive
Area: Arnavutköy Mh.
Address: Arnavutköy Bebek Cad. 71
34345 Istanbul Turkey
Phone: (0212) 2653269

#344
Yakup 2 Restaurant
Cuisines: Turkish
Average price: Modest
Area: Asmalı Mescit Mh.
Address: Asmalımescit Sok. No:35 D:37
34200 Istanbul Turkey
Phone: (0212) 2492925

#345
Kurufasülyeci Erzincanlı Ali Baba
Cuisines: Turkish
Average price: Modest
Area: Süleymaniye Mh.
Address: Prof. Sıddık Sami Onar Cad. No:11
34200 Istanbul Turkey
Phone: (0212) 5136219

#346
Ahırkapı Balıkçısı
Cuisines: Seafood
Average price: Expensive
Area: Sultan Ahmet Mh.
Address: Keresteci Hakkı Sk 12-52
34122 Istanbul Turkey
Phone: (0212) 5184988

#347
Güler Osmanlı Mutfağı
Cuisines: Turkish, Pita, Kebab
Average price: Modest
Area: Hasanpaşa Mh.
Address: Hasanpaşa Mh
34722 Istanbul Turkey
Phone: (0216) 3482245

#348
Öz Kilis Kebap ve Lahmacun Salonu
Cuisines: Kebab, Lahmacun
Average price: Modest
Area: Akşemsettin Mh.
Address: Bedrettin Simavi Sok. No: 5
34080 Istanbul Turkey
Phone: (0212) 5234457

#349
Virginia Angus
Cuisines: Burgers, Meatballs
Average price: Modest
Area: Halaskargazi Mh.
Address: Halaskargazi Mh.
34371 Istanbul Turkey
Phone: (0212) 2341525

#350
Revma Balık
Cuisines: Seafood
Average price: Expensive
Area: Arnavutköy Mh.
Address: No: 7
34283 Istanbul Turkey
Phone: (0212) 2635060

#351
Göksu Cafe
Cuisines: Coffee & Tea, Cafe
Average price: Modest
Area: Anadolu Hisarı Mh.
Address: Toplar Önü Sok. No: 5
34398 Istanbul Turkey
Phone: (0216) 3321637

#352
Unkapanı Pilavcısı & Kokoreç
Cuisines: Rice, Giblets
Average price: Inexpensive
Area: Kalenderhane Mh.
Address: No: 146 D: 3
34200 Istanbul Turkey
Phone: (0212) 5148343

#353
Meşhur Sedef Dönerci
Cuisines: Donairs, Burgers
Average price: Modest
Area: Binbirdirek Mh.
Address: Binbirdirek Mah.
34122 Istanbul Turkey
Phone: (0212) 5162420

#354
Aheste Pera
Cuisines: Turkish, Tapas Bar
Average price: Expensive
Area: Asmalı Mescit Mh.
Address: Meşrutiyet Cd.No: 107/F
34430 Istanbul Turkey
Phone: (0212) 2432633

#355
Sahrap Restaurant
Cuisines: Kebab, Turkish, Cafe
Average price: Expensive
Area: Asmalı Mescit Mh.
Address: Asmalı Mescit Mah.
34430 Istanbul Turkey
Phone: (0212) 2431616

#356
Çınaraltı Mangalbaşı
Cuisines: Barbeque, Turkish,
Do-It-Yourself Food
Average price: Expensive
Area: Altıntepe Mh.
Address: Kasaplar Çarşısı No: 6 D: 2
34087 Istanbul Turkey
Phone: (0216) 5184865

#357
Bursa Kebapçısı
Cuisines: Kebab
Average price: Modest
Area: Hüseyinağa Mh.
Address: Hüseyinağa Mah.
34250 Istanbul Turkey
Phone: (0212) 2499742

#358
Tacofit
Cuisines: Mexican
Average price: Modest
Area: Nisbetiye Mh.
Address: Nisbetiye Cad. No:42/A
34337 Istanbul Turkey
Phone: (0212) 2841117

#359
Çukurcuma'da Bahar
Cuisines: Turkish
Average price: Expensive
Area: Kuloğlu Mh.
Address: Kuloğlu Mah.
34250 Istanbul Turkey
Phone: (0212) 2445550

#360
Asia Chai Art
Cuisines: Coffee & Tea, Cafe
Average price: Modest
Area: 19 Mayıs Mh.
Address: Şemsettin Günaltay Cad.No:121
34736 Istanbul Turkey
Phone: (0216) 4450001

#361
Beyaz lokanta
Cuisines: Diners
Average price: Inexpensive
Area: Şehit Muhtar Mh.
Address: İstiklal Cad. İmam Adnan Sok.
No:10. 34250 Istanbul Turkey
Phone: (0212) 2927197

#362
Eat Box
Cuisines: Burgers, Sandwiches, American
Average price: Inexpensive
Area: Abbasağa Mh.
Address: Jandarma Mektebi Sok. No:1
34330 Istanbul Turkey
Phone: (0212) 3270123

#363
OD46
Cuisines: Creperies
Average price: Modest
Area: Caferağa Mh.
Address: Caferağa Mah.
34710 Istanbul Turkey
Phone: (0216) 3367284

#364
Ondo Dürüm
Cuisines: Turkish, Meatballs, Barbeque
Average price: Modest
Area: Karadolap Mh.
Address: Karadolap Mah.
34400 Istanbul Turkey
Phone: (0212) 4270505

#365
Karaköy Gümrük
Cuisines: Turkish, Mediterranean,
Breakfast & Brunch
Average price: Modest
Area: Kemankeş Karamustafa Paşa Mh.
Address: Kemankeş Karamustafa Paşa Mh.
34425 Istanbul Turkey
Phone: (0212) 2442252

#366
Ovalı
Cuisines: Turkish
Average price: Inexpensive
Area: Ihlamurkuyu Mh.
Address: Tepeüstü Mah.
34398 Istanbul Turkey
Phone: (0216) 6117373

#367
Çekirdek
Cuisines: Coffee & Tea, Cafe
Average price: Modest
Area: Caferağa Mh.
Address: Caferağa Mah.Şair Latifi Sok. No:9
34710 Istanbul Turkey
Phone: (0216) 3467700

#368
Go Mongo
Cuisines: Southern
Average price: Expensive
Area: Suadiye Mh.
Address: Plaj Yolu Sok. Suadiye Park A Blok
No: 18 D: 3 Istanbul Turkey
Phone: (0216) 4103223

#369
Trattoria Serenzo
Cuisines: Italian
Average price: Expensive
Area: Gayrettepe Mh.
Address: Vefa Bey Sok. No:25
34400 Istanbul Turkey
Phone: (0212) 2744410

#370
The Bosnjak Mutfak
Cuisines: Restaurants
Average price: Expensive
Area: Etiler Mh.
Address: Etiler Mh.
34337 Istanbul Turkey
Phone: (0212) 2870723

#371
Roka Balık
Cuisines: Seafood, Mediterranean, Bar
Average price: Modest
Area: Koşuyolu Mh.
Address: Koşuyolu Mh.
34718 Istanbul Turkey
Phone: (0216) 3397172

#372
ÇokÇok Thai Restaurant
Cuisines: Thai
Average price: Expensive
Area: Asmalı Mescit Mh.
Address: Meşrutiyet Cad. No:51/A
34400 Istanbul Turkey
Phone: (0212) 2926496

#373
Thales Rock
Cuisines: Bar, Cafe
Average price: Modest
Area: Katip Mustafa Çelebi Mh.
Address: Hasnungalip Sk. No: 5 K: 2
34250 Istanbul Turkey
Phone: (0212) 2923914

#374
Küçük Ev
Cuisines: Kebab, Turkish
Average price: Modest
Area: Topkapı Mh.
Address: No: 9
34200 Istanbul Turkey
Phone: (0212) 5323423

#375
Carl's Jr
Cuisines: Burgers, Fast Food
Average price: Inexpensive
Area: İçerenköy Mh.
Address: İçerenköy Carrefour Avm
Istanbul Turkey
Phone: (0212) 3801818

#376
Kurufasulyeci Ender Usta
Cuisines: Turkish
Average price: Modest
Area: Kavacık Mh.
Address: Kavacık Mah.
34810 Istanbul Turkey
Phone: (0216) 6801453

#377
Cafe Bunka
Cuisines: Japanese, Sushi Bar
Average price: Modest
Area: Şehit Muhtar Mh.
Address: Ana Çeşme Sok. No: 3
34435 Istanbul Turkey
Phone: (0212) 2933249

#378
Cibalikapı Balıkçısı
Cuisines: Seafood
Average price: Expensive
Area: Cibali Mh.
Address: No: 5
34200 Istanbul Turkey
Phone: (0212) 5332846

#379
Buhara 93
Cuisines: Turkish
Average price: Modest
Area: Sultan Ahmet Mh.
Address: Sultanahmet Mah.
34200 Istanbul Turkey
Phone: (0212) 5181511

#380
Backyard
Cuisines: Cafe, Coffee & Tea
Average price: Exclusive
Area: Bebek Mh.
Address: Otlukbeli Cad.Bebeköy Sok.
No: 4 Istanbul Turkey
Phone: (0212) 2871500

#381
Kebabi
Cuisines: Turkish
Average price: Expensive
Area: Gayrettepe Mh.
Address: No: 44 D: 3
34400 Istanbul Turkey
Phone: (0212) 2753522

#382
Falafel House
Cuisines: Middle Eastern, Falafel
Average price: Modest
Area: Kocatepe Mh.
Address: Şehit Muhtar Cad. No: 19/ A
34250 Istanbul Turkey
Phone: (0212) 2537730

#383
Amedros Cafe
Cuisines: Turkish, Seafood, Steakhouse
Average price: Modest
Area: Alemdar Mh.
Address: Divanyolu Cad. Hoca Rüstem Sok.
No: 7. 34200 Istanbul Turkey
Phone: (0212) 5228356

#384
360 İstanbul East
Cuisines: Mediterranean, Cafe, Coffee & Tea
Average price: Expensive
Area: Caferağa Mh.
Address: Doubletree By Hilton Moda
34550 Istanbul Turkey
Phone: (0216) 5424350

#385
Çanak Mangalda Kuru Fasülye
Cuisines: Turkish
Average price: Inexpensive
Area: Ayvansaray Mh.
Address: Karabaş Mah. Hisarönü Cad. No:1
34400 Istanbul Turkey
Phone: (0212) 6215835

#386
Sedona Concept
Cuisines: Bike Rentals, Cafe, Coffee & Tea
Average price: Modest
Area: Yeniköy Mh.
Address: Köybaşı Cad. No:136
34464 Istanbul Turkey
Phone: (0212) 2624444

#387
Baazen Tantuni
Cuisines: Turkish, Desserts, Kebab
Average price: Inexpensive
Area: Levent Mh.
Address: Levent Cad. No.1
34250 Istanbul Turkey
Phone: (0212) 2801515

#388
Develi Kalamış
Cuisines: Turkish
Average price: Expensive
Area: Fenerbahçe Mh.
Address: Münir Nurettin Selçuk Cad.
34726 Istanbul Turkey
Phone: (0216) 4189400

#389
Kaşıkçı Pilav
Cuisines: Turkish
Average price: Inexpensive
Area: Emniyetevleri Mh.
Address: Emniyetevler mah. Cem Sultan
Caddesi. No:5 / 4.Levent
34330 Istanbul Turkey
Phone: (0212) 3244929

#390
Akın Restoran
Cuisines: Turkish
Average price: Inexpensive
Area: Arap Cami Mh.
Address: Tersane Cad.120/A
34421 Istanbul Turkey
Phone: (0212) 2560007

#391
Özgür Şef Steakhouse
Cuisines: Steakhouse, Burgers
Average price: Expensive
Area: Barbaros Mh.
Address: Karanfil Sok. No: 6
34700 Istanbul Turkey
Phone: (0216) 6884343

#392
Sultan Teras Cafe
Cuisines: Cafe, Coffee & Tea
Average price: Modest
Area: Süleymaniye Mh.
Address: Süleymaniye Mah.
34200 Istanbul Turkey
Phone: (0212) 5143748

#393
Moda Meyhanesi
Cuisines: Tabernas
Average price: Modest
Area: Caferağa Mh.
Address: Caferağa Mah.
34710 Istanbul Turkey
Phone: (0216) 3370258

#394
Chalet Restaurant
Cuisines: Modern European
Average price: Expensive
Area: Vişnezade Mh.
Address: Swissotel The Bosphorus İstanbul
No: 2 Istanbul Turkey
Phone: (0212) 3261100

#395
Çakmak Kahvaltı Salonu
Cuisines: Breakfast & Brunch
Average price: Inexpensive
Area: Sinanpaşa Mh.
Address: Çelebioglu Sok.
34200 Istanbul Turkey
Phone: (0212) 2272565

#396
Ağa Kapısı
Cuisines: Coffee & Tea, Cafe
Average price: Modest
Area: Demirtaş Mh.
Address: Fetva Yokuşu Nazir İzzet Efendi
Sok. No: 11. 34200 Istanbul Turkey
Phone: (0212) 5195176

#397
Venge Restaurant
Cuisines: Turkish
Average price: Expensive
Area: Konaklar Mh.
Address: Akasyalı Sok. No: 2
34200 Istanbul Turkey
Phone: (0212) 2819383

#398
Venture Coffeeworks
Cuisines: Coffee & Tea, Cafe
Average price: Inexpensive
Area: Caferağa Mh.
Address: Caferağa Mh.
34710 Istanbul Turkey
Phone: (0532) 7230277

#399
Beşaltı Kirvem Tantuni & Künefe
Cuisines: Turkish, Barbeque
Average price: Inexpensive
Area: Kemankeş Karamustafa Paşa Mh.
Address: Mumhane Cd. No:35/B
34200 Istanbul Turkey
Phone: (0212) 2440347

#400
Fasuli
Cuisines: Turkish
Average price: Modest
Area: Kemankeş Karamustafa Paşa Mh.
Address: Kılıç Ali Paşa Mescidi Sok. No: 6
34200 Istanbul Turkey
Phone: (0212) 2436580

#401
Mano Burger
Cuisines: Fast Food, Burgers
Average price: Modest
Area: Caddebostan Mh.
Address: İskele Sk. No:14
34728 Istanbul Turkey
Phone: (0216) 3029444

#402
İki Kedi Cafe
Cuisines: Coffee & Tea, Cafe
Average price: Inexpensive
Area: Caferağa Mh.
Address: Dr. Esat Isik Cad. 9/ B
34710 Istanbul Turkey
Phone: (0216) 3470456

#403
Mezzaluna
Cuisines: Italian
Average price: Modest
Area: Harbiye Mh.
Address: No: 21
34400 Istanbul Turkey
Phone: (0212) 2313142

#404
Esmer Cafe
Cuisines: Italian
Average price: Modest
Area: Şehit Muhtar Mh.
Address: İstiklal Cad. No: 76
34250 Istanbul Turkey
Phone: (0212) 2455656

#405
Mahalle
Cuisines: Music Venues, Cafe, Cocktail Bar
Average price: Modest
Area: Teşvikiye Mh.
Address: Topağacı Mah.
34200 Istanbul Turkey
Phone: (0212) 2414873

#406
Çikolata Kahve
Cuisines: Coffee & Tea, Cafe
Average price: Modest
Area: Çengelköy Mh.
Address: Çengelköy Cd.
34680 Istanbul Turkey
Phone: (0216) 4222533

#407
Mums Cafe
Cuisines: Cafe, Coffee & Tea,
Breakfast & Brunch
Average price: Modest
Area: Kemankeş Karamustafa Paşa Mh.
Address: Kemankes Karamustafa Pasa Mh.
34200 Istanbul Turkey
Phone: (0212) 2459848

#408
Beer Hall
Cuisines: Beer, Wine & Spirits,
Gastropub, Fast Food
Average price: Modest
Area: Vişnezade Mh.
Address: Vişnezade Mah.
34357 Istanbul Turkey
Phone: (0212) 2196530

#409
Figaros Restaurant
Cuisines: Vegetarian
Average price: Modest
Area: Yeşilköy Mh.
Address: Demirci Çıkmazı Osman Gürer Sok.
No: 4 Istanbul Turkey
Phone: (0212) 5734383

#410
Hayri Usta
Cuisines: Turkish
Average price: Inexpensive
Area: Ayvansaray Mh.
Address: Katip Mustafa Çelebi Mah.
34087 Istanbul Turkey
Phone: (0212) 2493141

#411
Kiva Han
Cuisines: Turkish
Average price: Modest
Area: Şahkulu Mh.
Address: Galata Kulesi Meydanı No.4
34200 Istanbul Turkey
Phone: (0212) 2929898

#412
Palukçu Balık Lokantası
Cuisines: Seafood
Average price: Inexpensive
Area: Şehremini Mh.
Address: Büyük Saray Meydanı Cad. No: 13
34200 Istanbul Turkey
Phone: (0212) 5290872

#413
Hatay Antakya Mutfağı
Cuisines: Turkish, Mediterranean
Average price: Inexpensive
Area: Sinanpaşa Mh.
Address: Şair Nedim Cad. No:20
34200 Istanbul Turkey
Phone: (0212) 2362985

#414
Gani Gani Şark Sofrası
Cuisines: Turkish, Pita
Average price: Modest
Area: Evliya Çelebi Mh.
Address: Katip Mustafa Çelebi Mah.
Taksim Kuyu Sok. No: 11
34200 Istanbul Turkey
Phone: (0212) 2448401

#415
Casita
Cuisines: Turkish Ravioli, Homemade Food
Average price: Modest
Area: Nisbetiye Mh.
Address: Nispetiye Cad.
34337 Istanbul Turkey
Phone: (0212) 2637007

#416
Lokma
Cuisines: Mediterranean, Turkish, Bar
Average price: Modest
Area: Emniyettepe Mh.
Address: Santral Kampusu
34050 Istanbul Turkey
Phone: (0212) 3224822

#417
Bomonti Brasserie
Cuisines: Pubs, Brasseries, Turkish
Average price: Modest
Area: Mecidiye Mh.
Address: Mecidiye Mh.
34330 Istanbul Turkey
Phone: (0212) 2591955

#418
Bambi Cafe
Cuisines: Fast Food, Breakfast & Brunch
Average price: Inexpensive
Area: Hobyar Mh.
Address: Hobyar Mah.
34200 Istanbul Turkey
Phone: (0212) 5120808

#419
Marbella Cafe Restaurant
Cuisines: Seafood, Turkish,
Breakfast & Brunch
Average price: Expensive
Area: Küçük Ayasofya Mh.
Address: Küçük Ayasofya Mh.
34122 Istanbul Turkey
Phone: (0212) 6380969

#420
Büyük Erzurum Sofrası
Cuisines: Turkish
Average price: Modest
Area: Kordonboyu Mh.
Address: Kordonboyu Mah.
34860 Istanbul Turkey
Phone: (0216) 4884747

#421
Cunda Balık
Cuisines: Mediterranean, Seafood
Average price: Expensive
Area: Bostancı Mh.
Address: Köy Yolu Sok. No:6/1
34744 Istanbul Turkey
Phone: (0216) 3805989

#422
Mezzaluna
Cuisines: Italian
Average price: Inexpensive
Area: Pınar Mh.
Address: İstinyePark AVM
34460 Istanbul Turkey
Phone: (0212) 3455500

#423
Aliye Meyhane
Cuisines: Turkish, Music Venues
Average price: Expensive
Area: Cihangir Mh.
Address: Cihangir Cad.
34250 Istanbul Turkey
Phone: (0212) 2442373

#424
Hacıbaşar Kebap&Baklava
Cuisines: Turkish, Desserts
Average price: Modest
Area: Göztepe Mh.
Address: No: 48 Istanbul Turkey
Phone: (0216) 3607037

#425
The Hunger
Cuisines: Steakhouse, Turkish, American
Average price: Modest
Area: Esentepe Mh.
Address: Yıldız Posta Cad. Müşir Abdullah
Sok. No: 38 D: 1. 34200 Istanbul Turkey
Phone: (0212) 2883227

#426
Isis
Cuisines: Cafe, Coffee & Tea
Average price: Modest
Area: Caferağa Mh.
Address: Kadife Sok. No: 26
34200 Istanbul Turkey
Phone: (0216) 3497381

#427
Divan Brasserie Beyoğlu
Cuisines: Cafe, Brasseries
Average price: Expensive
Area: Tomtom Mh.
Address: Tomtom Mah.
34400 Istanbul Turkey
Phone: (0212) 2432481

#428
Nizam Pide & Sütlaç Salonu
Cuisines: Turkish, Pita, Soup
Average price: Modest
Area: Kamer Hatun Mh.
Address: Kalyoncu Kulluk Cad. No:13
34250 Istanbul Turkey
Phone: (0212) 2495501

#429
ROP Coffee
Cuisines: Coffee & Tea, Cafe
Average price: Inexpensive
Area: Caferağa Mh.
Address: Doktor Esat Işık Cd.
34710 Istanbul Turkey
Phone: (0505) 2139756

#430
Gina
Cuisines: Italian
Average price: Exclusive
Area: Esentepe Mh.
Address: Kanyon Alışveriş Merkezi No: 185
D: 164/A K: 1 Istanbul Turkey
Phone: (0212) 3535452

#431
Fasuli Lokantaları
Cuisines: Turkish
Average price: Modest
Area: Şehremini Mh.
Address: Murat Paşa Mah. Millet Cad.
Istanbul Turkey
Phone: (0212) 5865153

#432
Musafir Indian Restaurant
Cuisines: Indian
Average price: Modest
Area: Kocatepe Mh.
Address: Recep Paşa Cad. No:7/C
34716 Istanbul Turkey
Phone: (0212) 2352741

#433
Tarihi Cumhuriyet İşkembe Salonu
Cuisines: Turkish, Soup, Giblets
Average price: Inexpensive
Area: Hüseyinağa Mh.
Address: Hüseyin Ağa Mah. Istanbul Turkey
Phone: (0212) 2927097

#434
Dai Pera Istanbul Cuisine
Cuisines: Turkish
Average price: Modest
Area: Tomtom Mh.
Address: Yeni Çarşı Cad. No: 54
34433 Istanbul Turkey
Phone: (0212) 2528099

#435
Konyali Restaurant
Cuisines: Turkish
Average price: Expensive
Area: Cankurtaran Mh.
Address: Cankurtaran Mah.
34122 Istanbul Turkey
Phone: (0212) 5139696

#436
Sabırtaşı Restoran
Cuisines: Turkish Ravioli, Meatballs,
Homemade Food
Average price: Inexpensive
Area: Asmalı Mescit Mh.
Address: İstiklal Cad. No:112
34430 Istanbul Turkey
Phone: (0212) 2448226

#437
Bilice Kebap
Cuisines: Kebab
Average price: Modest
Area: Asmalı Mescit Mh.
Address: Asmalımescit Mah.
34200 Istanbul Turkey
Phone: (0212) 2444447

#438
Kahve Dünyası
Cuisines: Coffee & Tea, Cafe
Average price: Inexpensive
Area: Büyükada-Nizam Mh.
Address: Nizam Mah.
34970 Istanbul Turkey
Phone: (0216) 3828399

#439
Kahve Dünyası
Cuisines: Coffee & Tea, Cafe
Average price: Modest
Area: Ömer Avni Mh.
Address: Meclisi Mebusan Cad.
34420 Istanbul Turkey
Phone: (0212) 2931206

#440
Tükkan
Cuisines: Italian, Cafe, Coffee & Tea
Average price: Modest
Area: Kemankeş Karamustafa Paşa Mh.
Address: Kemankeş Karamustafa Paşa Mah.
34200 Istanbul Turkey
Phone: (0212) 2453131

#441
Gran Karakoy
Cuisines: Cafe, Coffee & Tea
Average price: Modest
Area: Kemankeş Karamustafa Paşa Mh.
Address: Kemankeş Mah.
34200 Istanbul Turkey
Phone: (0212) 2444544

#442
Meal Box
Cuisines: Homemade Food
Average price: Modest
Area: Rüzgarlıbahçe Mh.
Address: Rüzgarlıbahçe Mah. Atatürk Cad.
34805 Istanbul Turkey
Phone: (0216) 4250102

#443
Cafe Post Office
Cuisines: Cafe, Coffee & Tea
Average price: Inexpensive
Area: Firuzağa Mh.
Address: Kılıç Ali Paşa Mah.
34425 Istanbul Turkey
Phone: (0212) 2439061

#444
İskele Restaurant
Cuisines: Seafood
Average price: Exclusive
Area: Rumeli Hisarı Mh.
Address: Yahya Kemal Cad. No: 1
34398 Istanbul Turkey
Phone: (0212) 2632997

#445
Tuğra Restaurant
Cuisines: Turkish
Average price: Exclusive
Area: Yıldız Mh.
Address: Çırağan Caddesi No 32
34200 Istanbul Turkey
Phone: (0212) 3264646

#446
Pide Sun
Cuisines: Pita
Average price: Modest
Area: Caferağa Mh.
Address: Moda Cad.
34710 Istanbul Turkey
Phone: (0216) 3473155

#447
Asmakat Ev Yemekleri
Cuisines: Cafe, Homemade Food
Average price: Inexpensive
Area: Caferağa Mh.
Address: Dr. Esat Işık Cad. No: 27
34710 Istanbul Turkey
Phone: (0216) 3304794

#448
Fornello
Cuisines: Pizza, Italian
Average price: Modest
Area: Caferağa Mh.
Address: Serasker Cad. No: 14
34200 Istanbul Turkey
Phone: (0216) 4496449

#449
Göze Terascafe
Cuisines: Coffee & Tea, Cafe
Average price: Modest
Area: İstinye Mh.
Address: Carrefour Express
Istanbul Turkey
Phone: (0212) 2713040

#450
Karabatak
Cuisines: Coffee & Tea, Cafe, Sandwiches
Average price: Modest
Area: Kemankeş Karamustafa Paşa Mh.
Address: Kara Mustafa Paşa Mah.
34425 Istanbul Turkey
Phone: (0212) 2436993

#451
Nişantaşı Başköşe
Cuisines: Turkish, Bar, Kebab
Average price: Expensive
Area: Harbiye Mh.
Address: Bronz Sk. No:5
34367 Istanbul Turkey
Phone: (0212) 2303868

#452
Mavi Restaurant
Cuisines: Turkish, Seafood
Average price: Expensive
Area: Heybeliada Mh.
Address: Yalı Cad. No: 23
34975 Istanbul Turkey
Phone: (0216) 3510128

#453
Göztepe Dönercisi
Cuisines: Turkish
Average price: Inexpensive
Area: Feneryolu Mh.
Address: No: 136 D: 1 Istanbul Turkey
Phone: (0216) 5671476

#454
Meat & Meet Kasap Dursun
Cuisines: Steakhouse
Average price: Modest
Area: Merkez Mh.
Address: Silahşör Cad. No 24
34250 Istanbul Turkey
Phone: (0212) 2342434

#455
Ovalı Konya Mutfağı
Cuisines: Turkish, Pita
Average price: Modest
Area: Ihlamurkuyu Mh.
Address: E-5 Ankara Asfaltı Yanyol
34956 Istanbul Turkey
Phone: (0216) 4887979

#456
Ops Cafe
Cuisines: Coffee & Tea, Cafe, Cafeteria
Average price: Modest
Area: Kemankeş Karamustafa Paşa Mh.
Address: Mumhane Cad. No: 45 / B
34200 Istanbul Turkey
Phone: (0212) 2450288

#457
Gönül Kahvesi
Cuisines: Coffee & Tea, Cafe
Average price: Inexpensive
Area: Balabanağa Mh.
Address: Balabanağa Mah.Ordu Cad.
34134 Istanbul Turkey
Phone: (0212) 5225685

#458
Brunelle
Cuisines: French, Mediterranean,
Breakfast & Brunch
Average price: Expensive
Area: Caferağa Mh.
Address: Hülya Sok. No: 5
34710 Istanbul Turkey
Phone: (0216) 3382561

#459
Borsam Taş Fırın
Cuisines: Pita, Lahmacun
Average price: Inexpensive
Area: Caferağa Mh.
Address: Caferağa Mah.
34718 Istanbul Turkey
Phone: (0216) 3370504

#460
Florya Sosyal Tesisleri
Cuisines: Turkish
Average price: Modest
Area: Yeşilyurt Mh.
Address: No: 1
34149 Istanbul Turkey
Phone: (0212) 6631867

#461
Big Chefs
Cuisines: Coffee & Tea, Cafe, Brasseries
Average price: Modest
Area: Barbaros Mh.
Address: My Prestige Binası
34776 Istanbul Turkey
Phone: (0216) 6884288

#462
Adanalı Kebapçı Şenol Kolcuoğlu
Cuisines: Turkish, Barbeque
Average price: Expensive
Area: Çınar Mh.
Address: Çınar Mah.
34865 Istanbul Turkey
Phone: (0216) 4893434

#463
FerahFeza
Cuisines: Mediterranean, Cafe, Coffee & Tea
Average price: Exclusive
Area: Kemankeş Karamustafa Paşa Mh.
Address: Kemankeş Cd. No 31
34200 Istanbul Turkey
Phone: (0212) 2435154

#464
Mitani
Cuisines: Bar, Cafe, Coffee & Tea
Average price: Modest
Area: Cankurtaran Mh.
Address: Akbiyik Cad.
3434122 Istanbul Turkey
Phone: (0530) 5802782

#465
Karpi Pide
Cuisines: Pita, Meatballs
Average price: Modest
Area: Beylerbeyi Mh.
Address: İskele Cad.
34676 Istanbul Turkey
Phone: (0216) 4224444

#466
Aida Vino e Cucina
Cuisines: Italian, Mediterranean
Average price: Expensive
Area: Caferağa Mh.
Address: Caferağa Mh. Moda Cad.
34710 Istanbul Turkey
Phone: (0216) 9690480

#467
Bambi Cafe
Cuisines: Fast Food, Donairs
Average price: Inexpensive
Area: Katip Mustafa Çelebi Mh.
Address: Sıraselviler Cad. No: 2
34250 Istanbul Turkey
Phone: (0212) 2932121

#468
Zalatta
Cuisines: Salad, Turkish
Average price: Modest
Area: Caferağa Mh.
Address: Muhurdar Cad. No:31/A
34714 Istanbul Turkey
Phone: (0216) 7002121

#469
Faros Old City Restaurant
Cuisines: Turkish, Bar, Kebab
Average price: Modest
Area: Alemdar Mh.
Address: Divanyolu Cad. No:76
34122 Istanbul Turkey
Phone: (0212) 5139113

#470
Bütme Evi
Cuisines: Fast Food, Gozleme, Soup
Average price: Inexpensive
Area: Caferağa Mh.
Address: Caferağa Mah.
34200 Istanbul Turkey
Phone: (0216) 4149775

#471
Gül Pastanesi
Cuisines: Desserts, Cafe, Bakeries
Average price: Modest
Area: Fulya Mh.
Address: Fulya Mh.
34394 Istanbul Turkey
Phone: (0212) 2179155

#472
Erenler Nargile ve Çay Bahçesi
Cuisines: Coffee & Tea, Hookah Bar, Cafe
Average price: Inexpensive
Area: Beyazıt Mh.
Address: Yeniçeriler Cd. No:36/28
34860 Istanbul Turkey
Phone: (0212) 5118853

#473
Adana Dostlar Kebapçısı
Cuisines: Kebab
Average price: Expensive
Area: Barbaros Mh.
Address: Barbaros Mah.
34100 Istanbul Turkey
Phone: (0216) 4729093

#474
Bodrum Mantı & Cafe
Cuisines: Turkish Ravioli, Cafe
Average price: Modest
Area: Arnavutköy Mh.
Address: Arnavutköy 1. Cad. No: 111
34538 Istanbul Turkey
Phone: (0212) 2632918

#475
Havuzlu Restaurant
Cuisines: Turkish
Average price: Modest
Area: Beyazıt Mh.
Address: Gani Çelebi Sok. No: 3
Istanbul Turkey
Phone: (0212) 5273346

#476
Meşhur Menemenci
Cuisines: Turkish, Breakfast & Brunch
Average price: Inexpensive
Area: Osmanağa Mh.
Address: Osmanağa Mh.
34200 Istanbul Turkey
Phone: (0216) 3366308

#477
Sakar Zeybek
Cuisines: Seafood, Turkish, Tapas Bar
Average price: Modest
Area: Koşuyolu Mh.
Address: Koşuyolu Mh.
34660 Istanbul Turkey
Phone: (0216) 3401008

#478
Palma d'Oro
Cuisines: Italian
Average price: Modest
Area: Suadiye Mh.
Address: Kazım Özalp Sok. No: 50
34740 Istanbul Turkey
Phone: (0216) 3632110

#479
Masa Restaurant
Cuisines: Turkish, Cafe, Coffee & Tea
Average price: Expensive
Area: Pınar Mh.
Address: İstinye Park AVM
34075 Istanbul Turkey
Phone: (0212) 3455323

#480
Gazebo
Cuisines: Cafe, Coffee & Tea
Average price: Expensive
Area: Yeniköy Mh.
Address: Köybaşı Cad. No: 125
34464 Istanbul Turkey
Phone: (0212) 2998487

#481
Müşterek Meyhane
Cuisines: Beer, Wine & Spirits,
Tabernas, Music Venues
Average price: Modest
Area: Şehit Muhtar Mh.
Address: Sehit Muhtar Mah.
34435 Istanbul Turkey
Phone: (0555) 7186559

#482
Müessese
Cuisines: Cafe, Coffee & Tea
Average price: Inexpensive
Area: Mecidiye Mh.
Address: Mecidiye Mah.
34
347 Istanbul Turkey
Phone: (0212) 2580059

#483
Tom's Kitchen
Cuisines: British, Breakfast & Brunch, Bar
Average price: Expensive
Area: Nisbetiye Mh.
Address: Zorlu Center
34340 Istanbul Turkey
Phone: (0212) 3536677

#484
Çerkezo
Cuisines: Fast Food
Average price: Modest
Area: Teşvikiye Mh.
Address: Teşvikiye Cad.
34400 Istanbul Turkey
Phone: (0212) 2608587

#485
Dürümce
Cuisines: Fast Food
Average price: Inexpensive
Area: Yıldız Mh.
Address: Mecidiye Mh.
34330 Istanbul Turkey
Phone: (0212) 2594924

#486
Cookshop
Cuisines: Restaurants
Average price: Modest
Area: Ataköy 1. Mh.
Address: Galleria Alışveriş Merkezi No: 6 D:
13 Istanbul Turkey
Phone: (0212) 5601811

#487
The Winston Brasserie
Cuisines: Brasseries, Cafe, Coffee & Tea
Average price: Modest
Area: Vişnezade Mh.
Address: Şair Nedim Cad. No: 3
34692 Istanbul Turkey
Phone: (0212) 2599919

#488
Develi Ataşehir
Cuisines: Kebab
Average price: Expensive
Area: Ataşehir Atatürk Mh.
Address: Vedat Günyol Cad. No: 9
34758 Istanbul Turkey
Phone: (0216) 5756868

#489
İntiba Döner
Cuisines: Kebab, Donairs
Average price: Modest
Area: Rüzgarlıbahçe Mh.
Address: Rüzgarlıbahçe Mah.
34660 Istanbul Turkey
Phone: (0216) 3314105

#490
Big Chef's Kanyon AVM
Cuisines: Brasseries, Cafe, Coffee & Tea
Average price: Modest
Area: Esentepe Mh.
Address: Kanyon AVM
34200 Istanbul Turkey
Phone: (0212) 3530707

#491
Agapia Garden
Cuisines: Turkish
Average price: Modest
Area: Caferağa Mh.
Address: Bahariye Cad. Miralay Nazım Sok.
No: 10. 34718 Istanbul Turkey
Phone: (0216) 4183636

#492
Bahçede Sinek Kafe
Cuisines: Coffee & Tea, Cafe
Average price: Modest
Area: Büyükada-Maden Mh.
Address: Maden Mah. Yılmaztürk Cad.
34970 Istanbul Turkey
Phone: (0216) 3823578

#493
Pişi Breakfast & Burger
Cuisines: Breakfast & Brunch,
Burgers, Turkish
Average price: Inexpensive
Area: Sinanpaşa Mh.
Address: Sinanpaşa Mah.
34353 Istanbul Turkey
Phone: (0212) 3277190

#494
Pepo Cafe & Restaurant
Cuisines: Turkish, Steakhouse
Average price: Modest
Area: Bereketzade Mh.
Address: Bereketzade Mh.
34400 Istanbul Turkey
Phone: (0212) 2451696

#495
Parantez Deli
Cuisines: Wine Bar, Delis
Average price: Modest
Area: Kocatepe Mh.
Address: Lamartin Cad.No: 4
34400 Istanbul Turkey
Phone: (0212) 2562603

#496
Sur Balık Restaurant
Cuisines: Seafood
Average price: Expensive
Area: Sultan Ahmet Mh.
Address: No: 18 Istanbul Turkey
Phone: (0212) 5175303

#497
Mekan Restaurant
Cuisines: Turkish
Average price: Expensive
Area: Tomtom Mh.
Address: Tom Tom Mh.
34200 Istanbul Turkey
Phone: (0212) 2526052

#498
Chinese & Sushi Express
Cuisines: Chinese, Sushi Bar
Average price: Expensive
Area: Kozyatağı Mh.
Address: Kozzy AVM
34710 Istanbul Turkey
Phone: (0216) 6580199

#499
Edebiyat Kiraathanesi
Cuisines: Cafe, Turkish, Coffee & Tea
Average price: Inexpensive
Area: Alemdar Mh.
Address: Divanyolu Cad. No: 14
34200 Istanbul Turkey
Phone: (0212) 5149068

#500
Sahan
Cuisines: Turkish
Average price: Expensive
Area: Suadiye Mh.
Address: Bağdat Cad.
34710 Istanbul Turkey
Phone: (0216) 3621919

Printed in Great Britain
by Amazon

64926886R00031